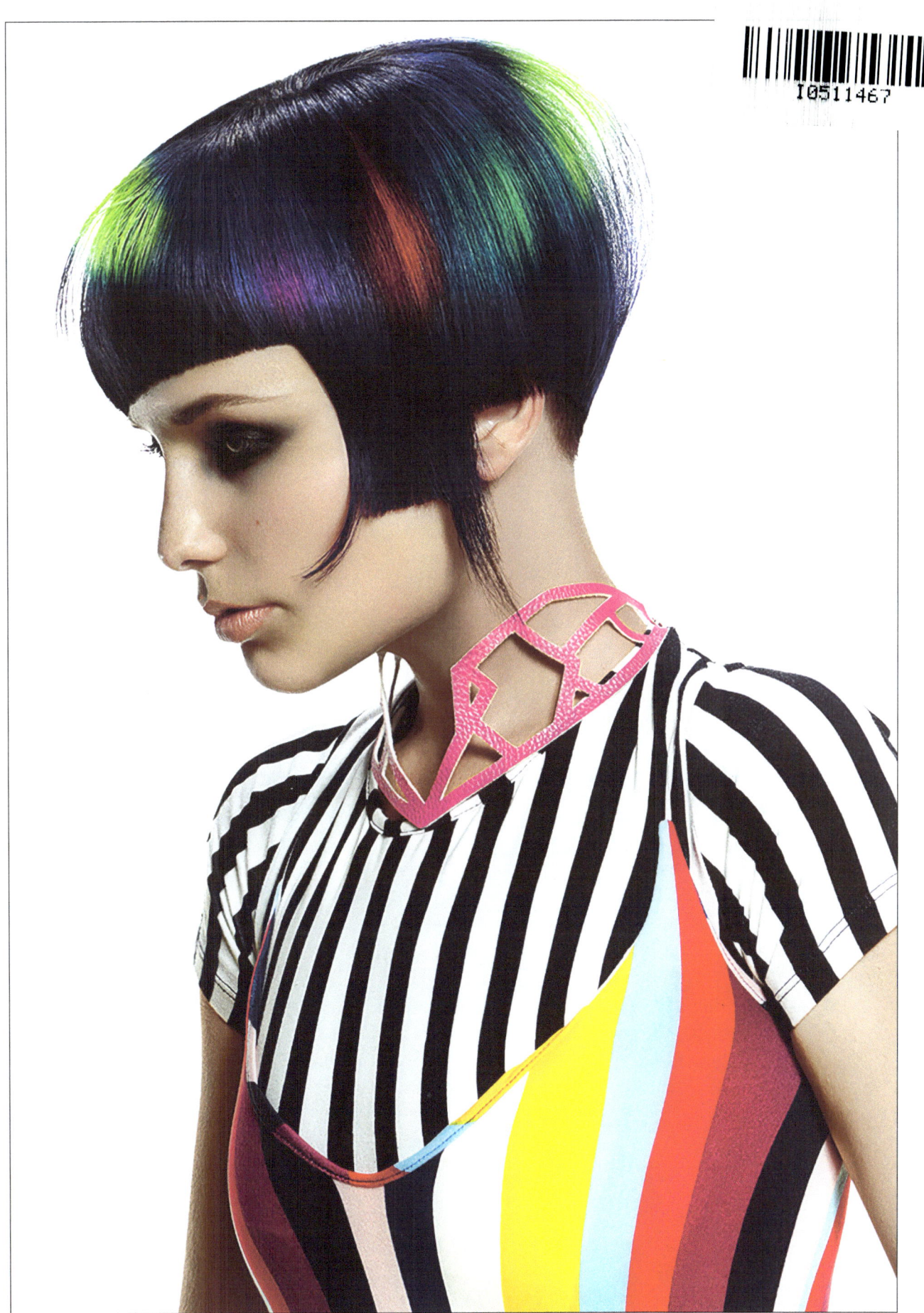

Hair: Chrystofer Benson Team - Make-up: Danielle Donahue - Photography: John Rawson

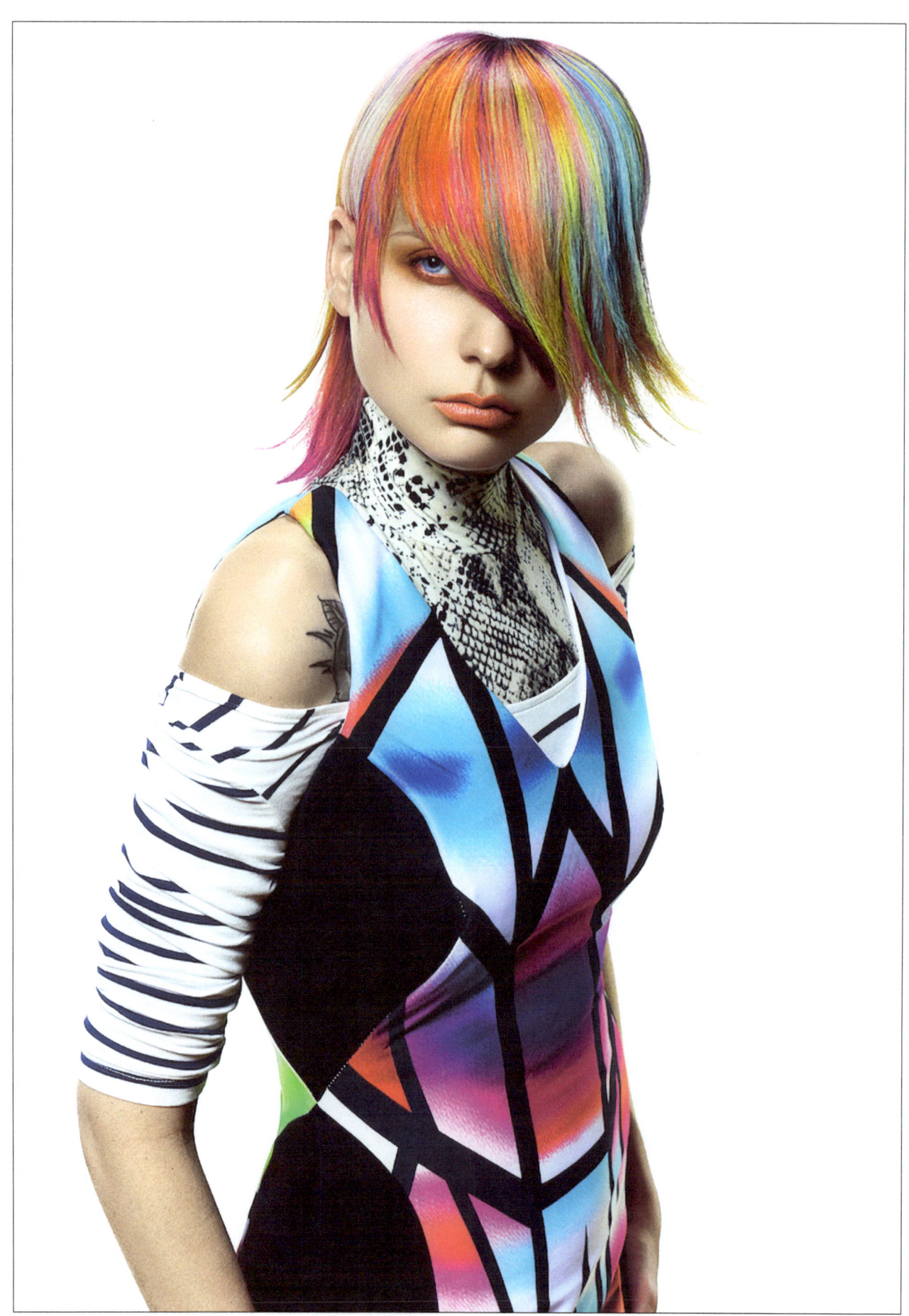

Hair: Chrystofer Benson Team - Make-up: Danielle Donahue - Photography: John Rawson

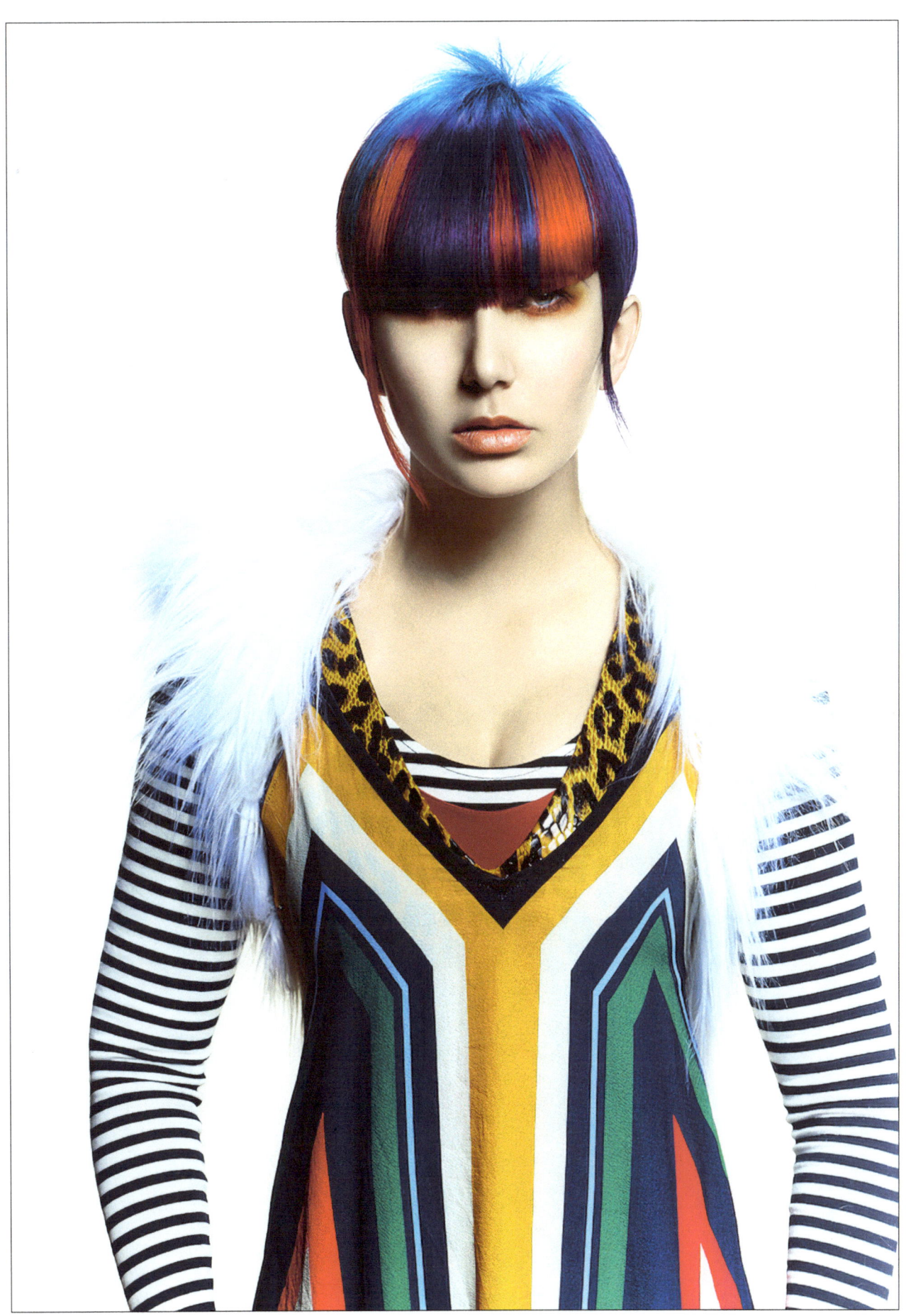

Hair: Chrystofer Benson Team - Make-up: Danielle Donahue - Photography: John Rawson

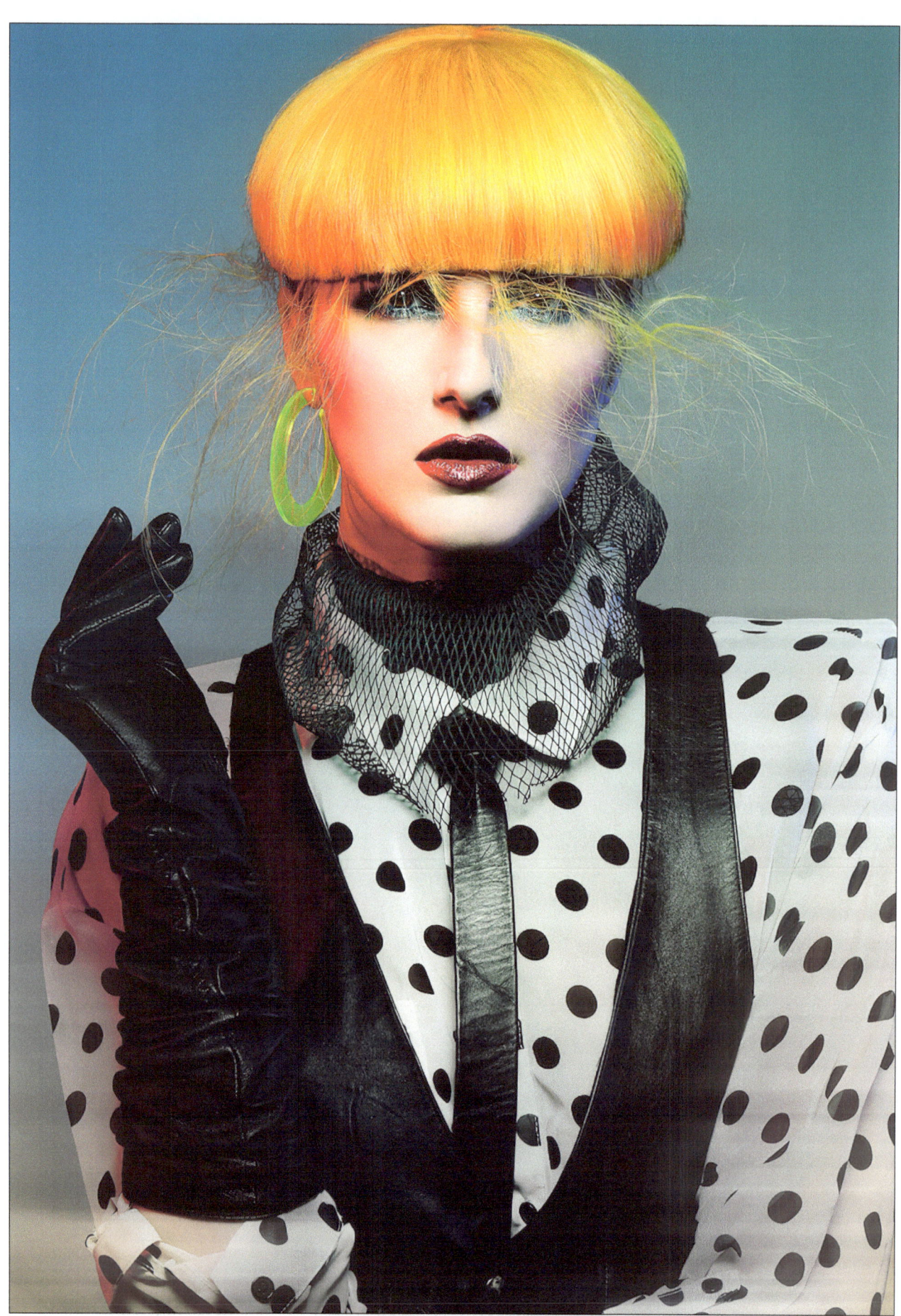

Hair: Julie Vriesinga - Make-up: Florencia Taylor - Photography: Paula Tizzard

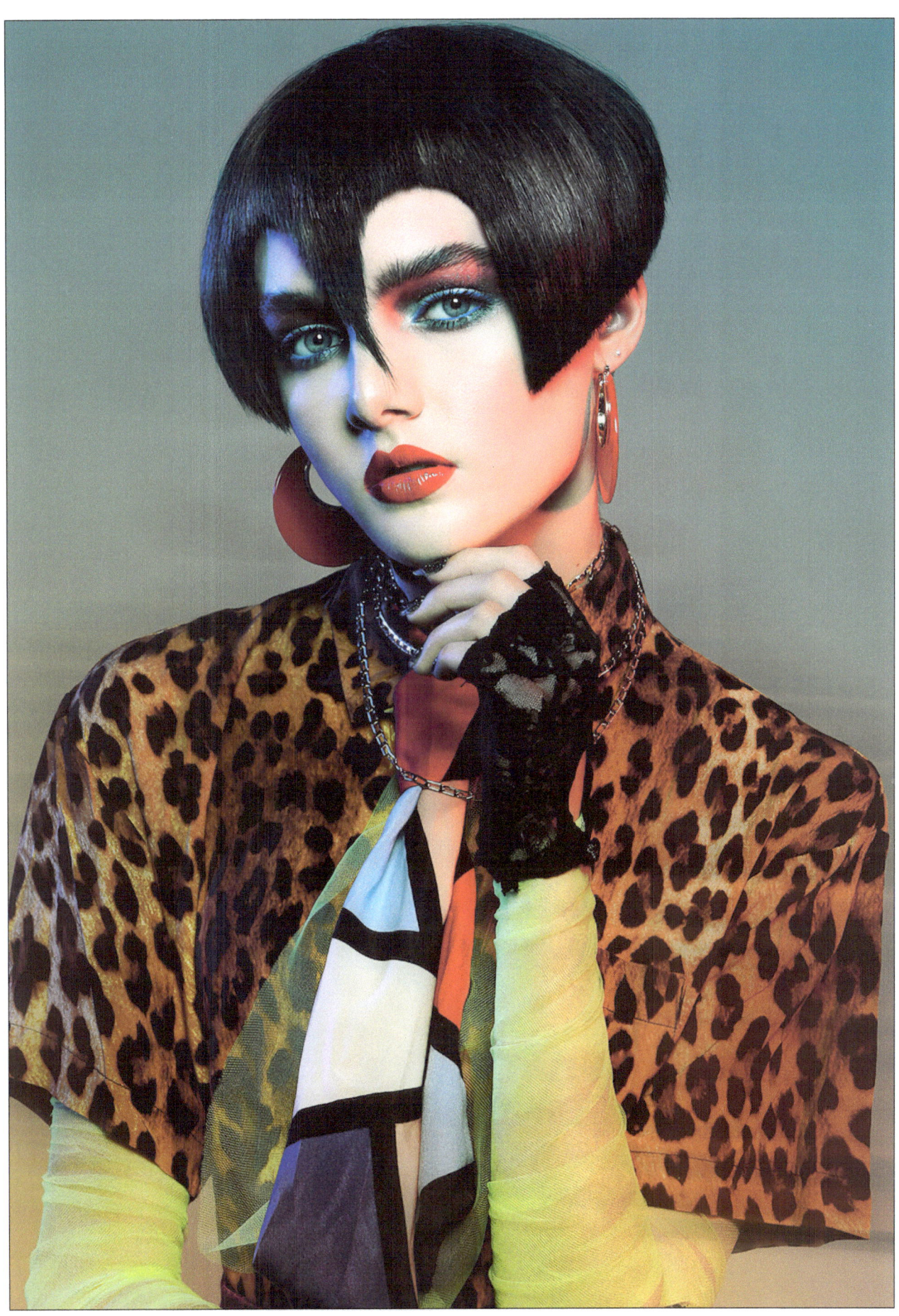

Hair: Julie Vriesinga - Make-up: Florencia Taylor - Photography: Paula Tizzard

ICON COLLECTION

Classic silhouettes are contrasted with modern grooming and technical detail, then teamed with pared-back fashion styling that lets the hair take centre stage.

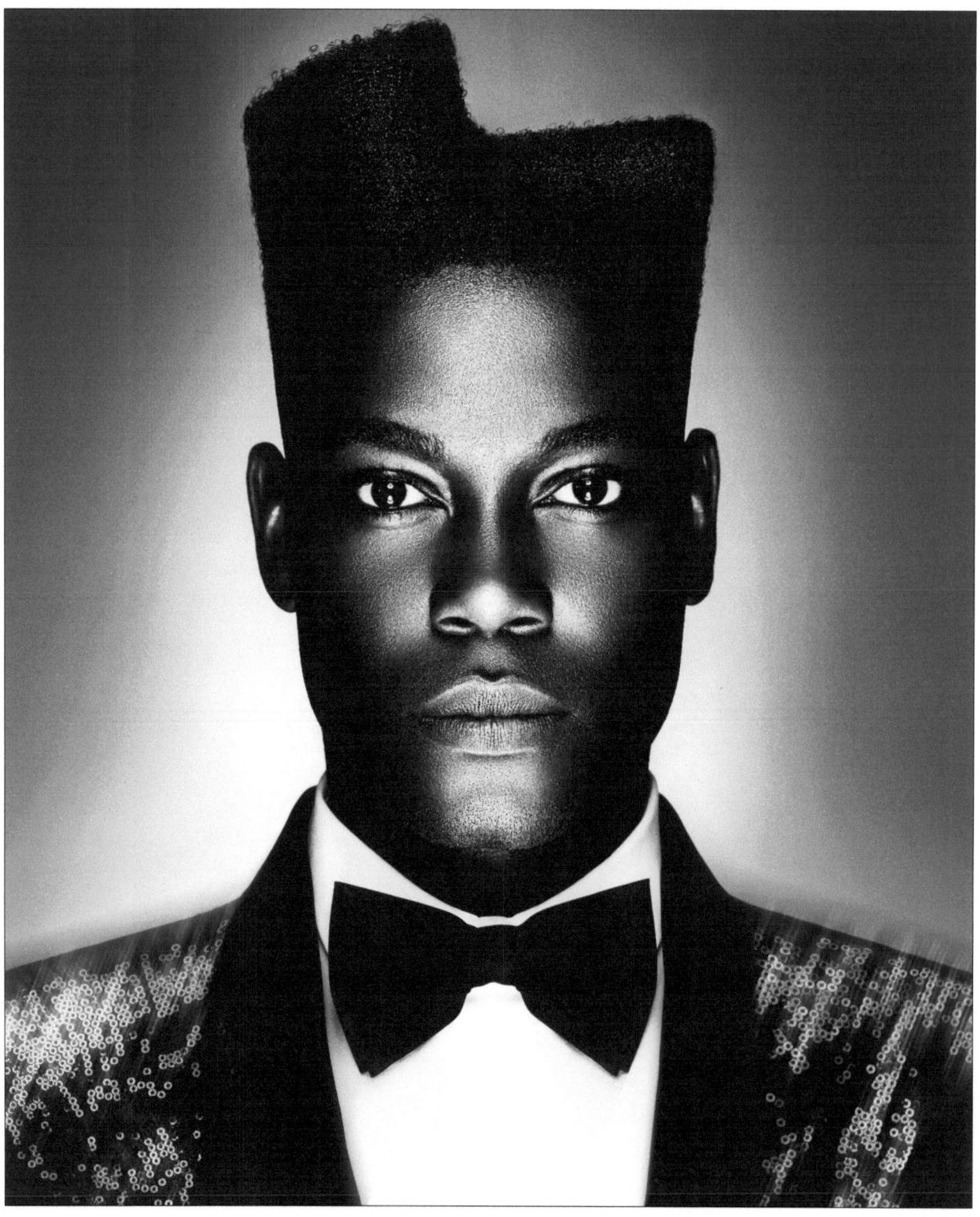

Hair: Andrea Giles & Terri Kay - Make-up: Clare Read - Styling: Bernard Connolly - Photography: Richard Miles

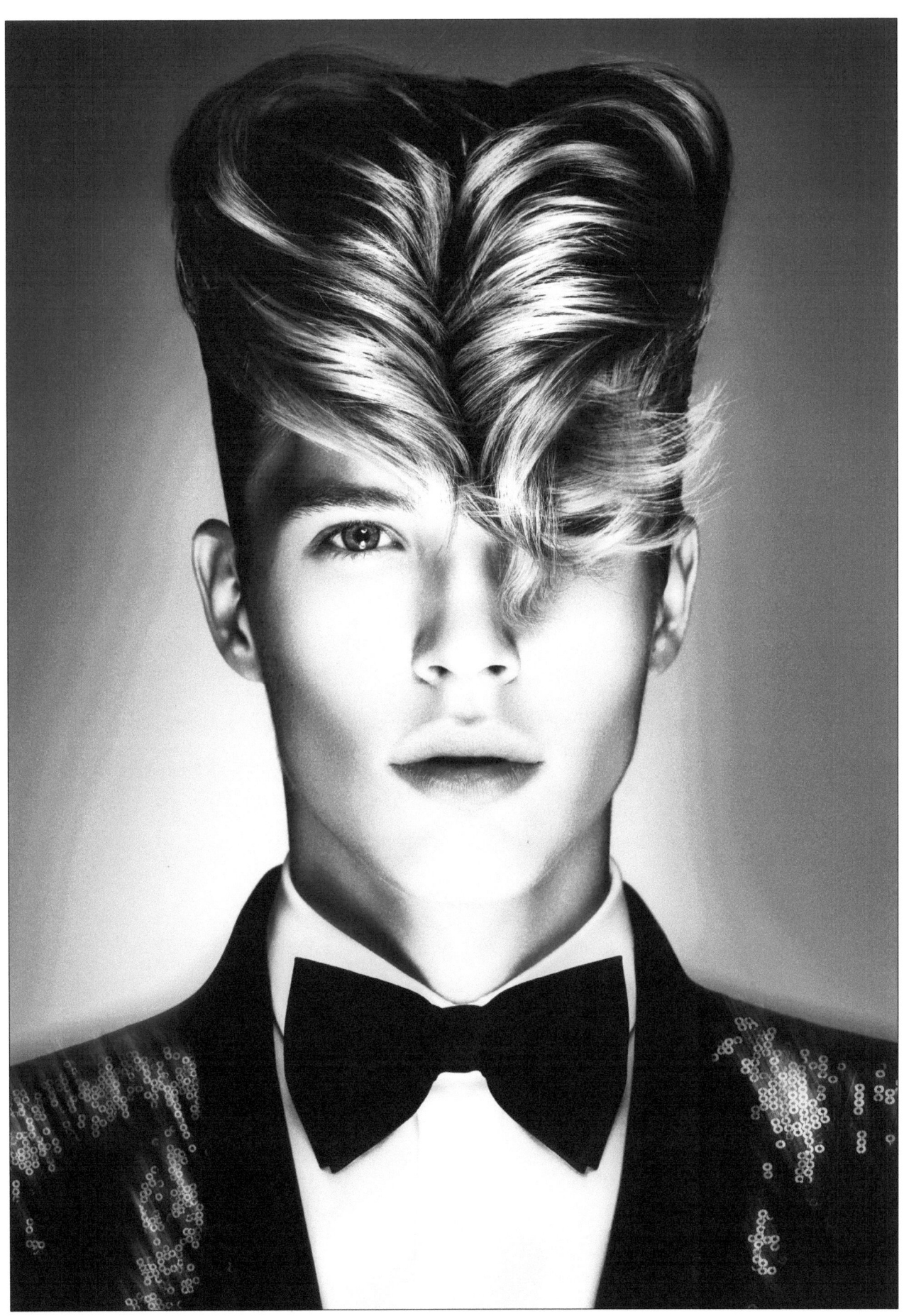

Hair: Andrea Giles & Terri Kay - Make-up: Clare Read - Styling: Bernard Connolly - Photography: Richard Miles

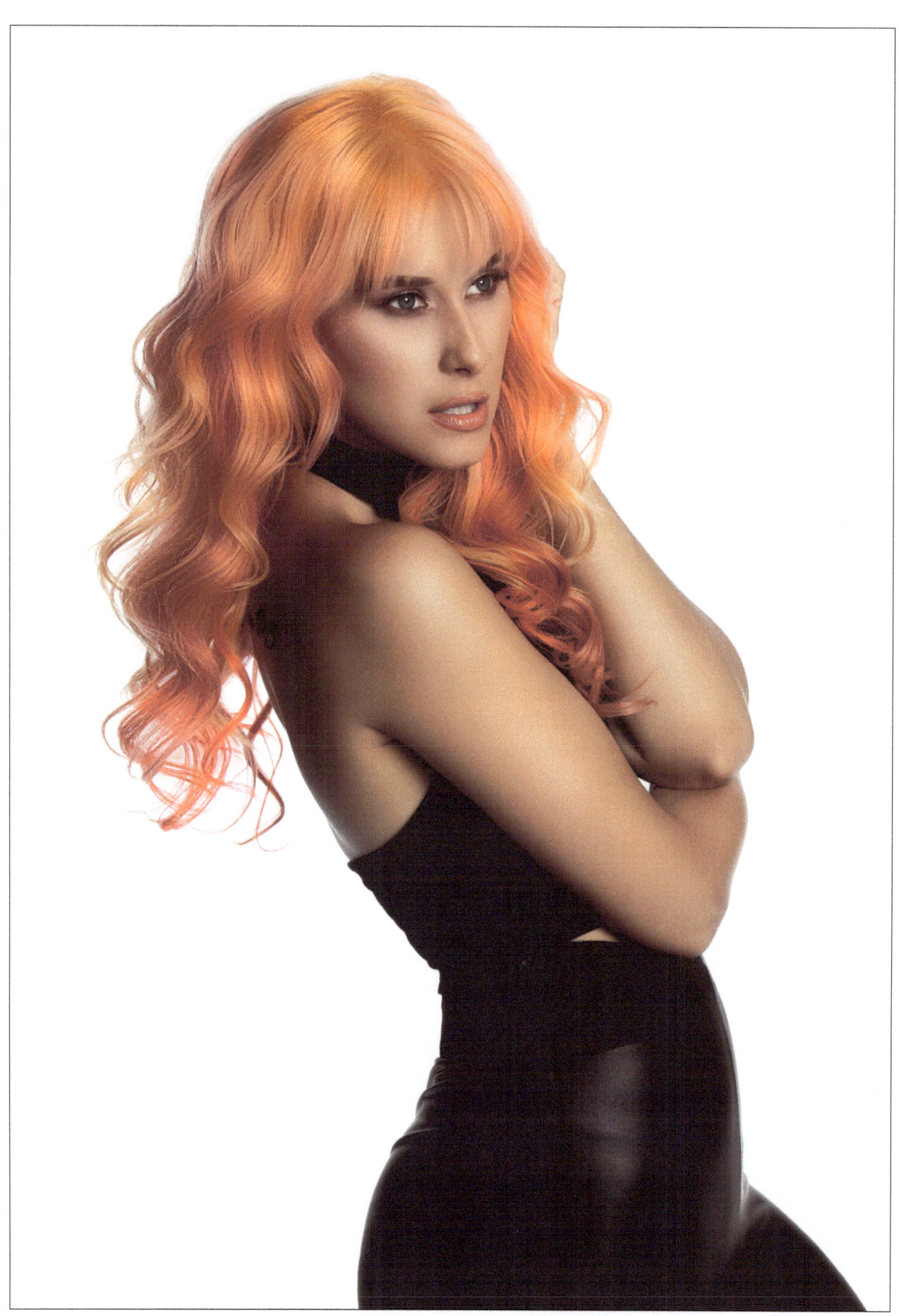

Hair: Anna Cantu & Rocky Vitelli - Make-up: Alberto Oz Caleb & Ashley Reyna - Photography: Mohammed Ghanayem

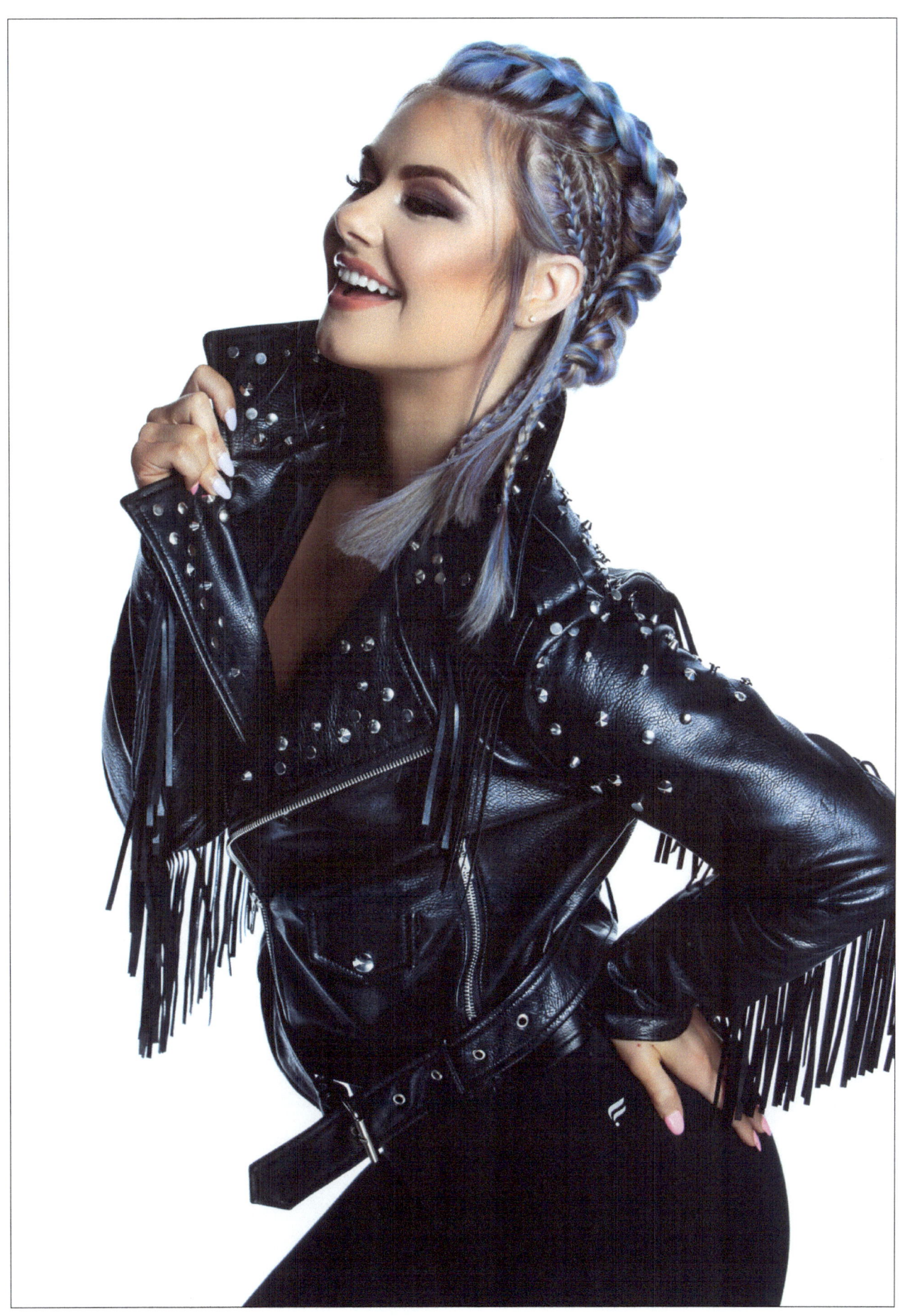

Hair: Anna Cantu & Rocky Vitelli - Make-up: Alberto Oz Caleb & Ashley Reyna - Photography: Mohammed Ghanayem

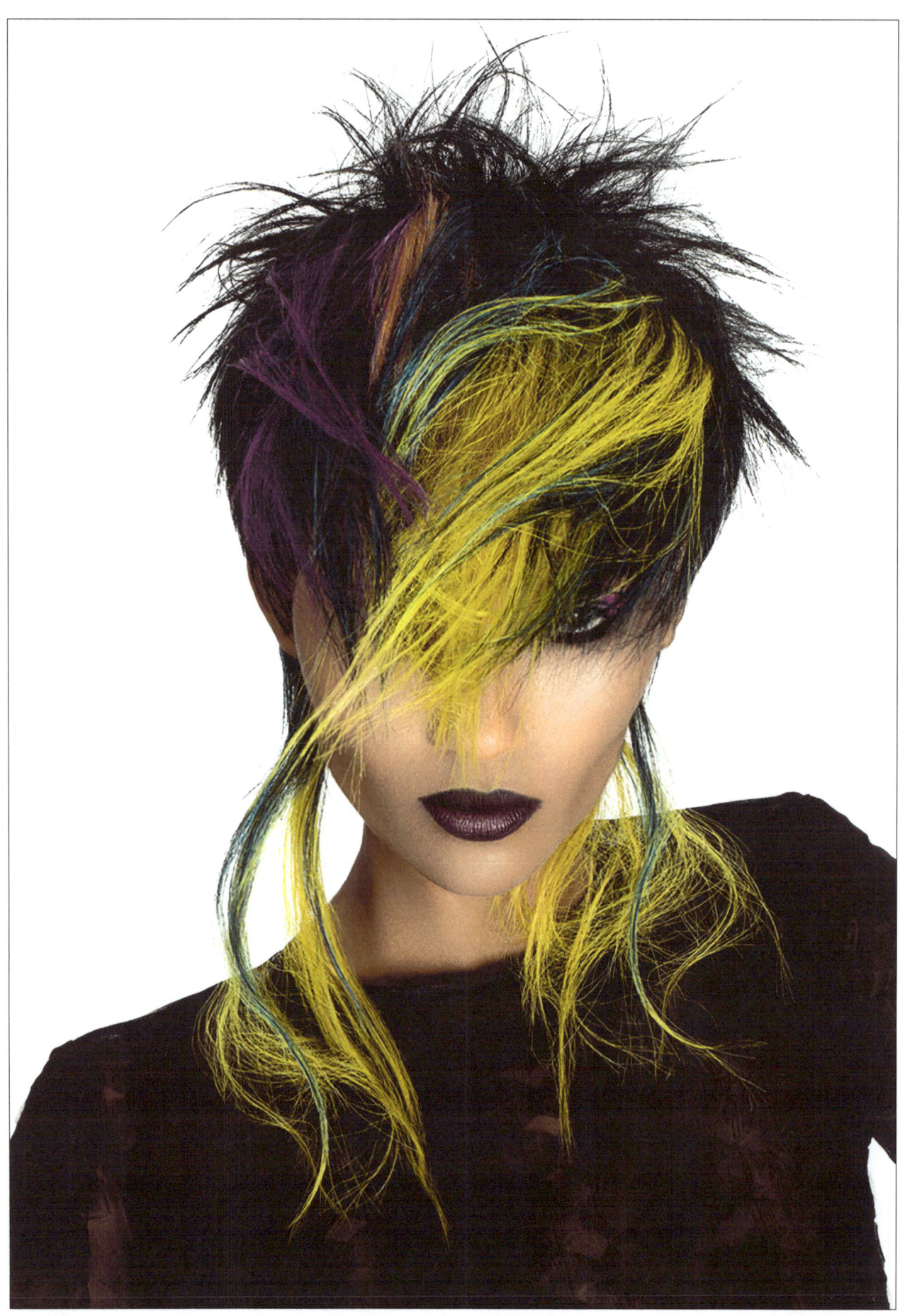

Hair: Genia Church - Make-up: Walter Obal - Photography: Damien Carney

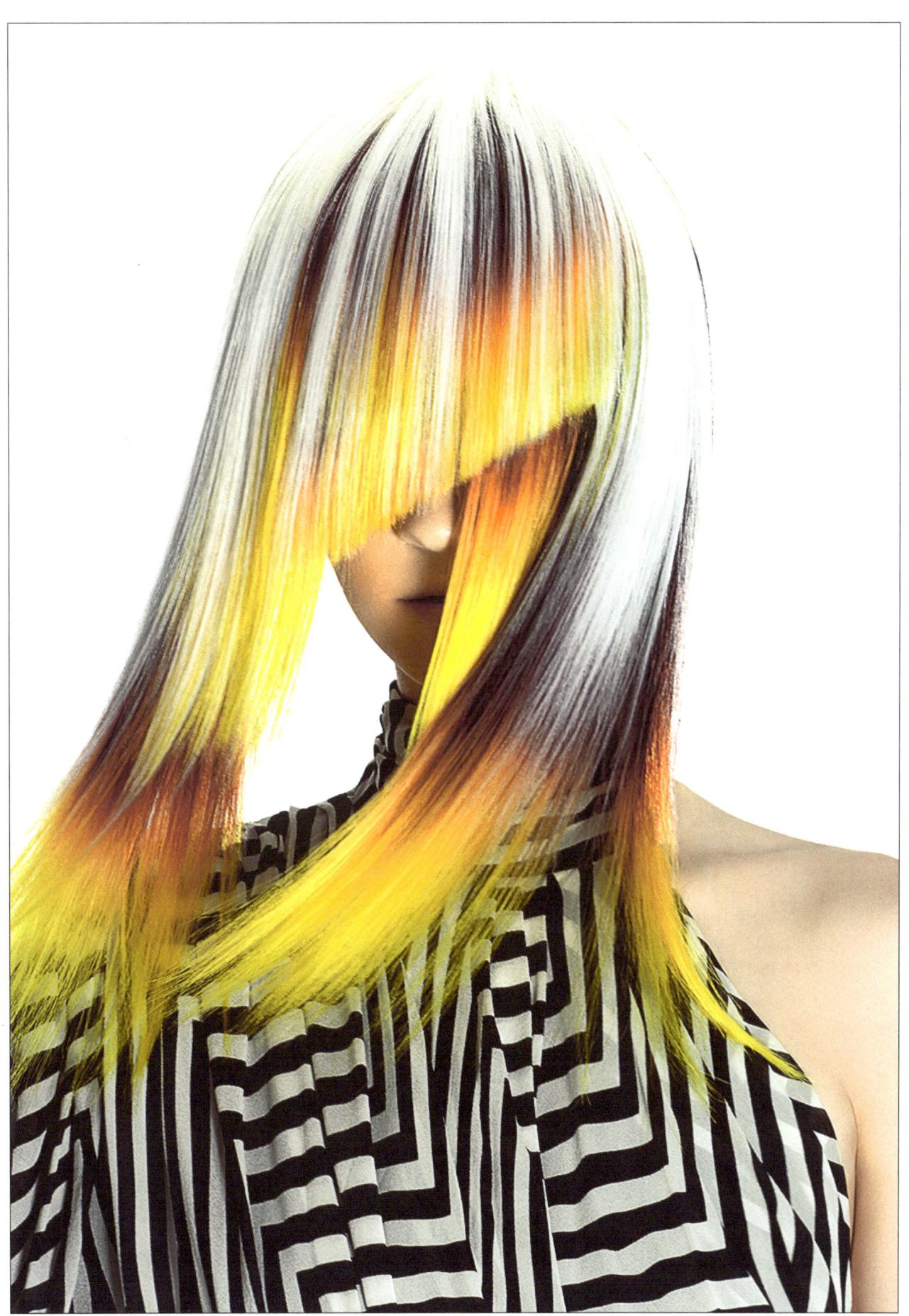

Hair: Genia Church - Make-up: Walter Obal - Photography: Damien Carney

YOUNGER GENERATION

Classic silhouettes are contrasted with modern grooming and technical detail, then teamed with pared-back fashion styling that lets the hair take centre stage.

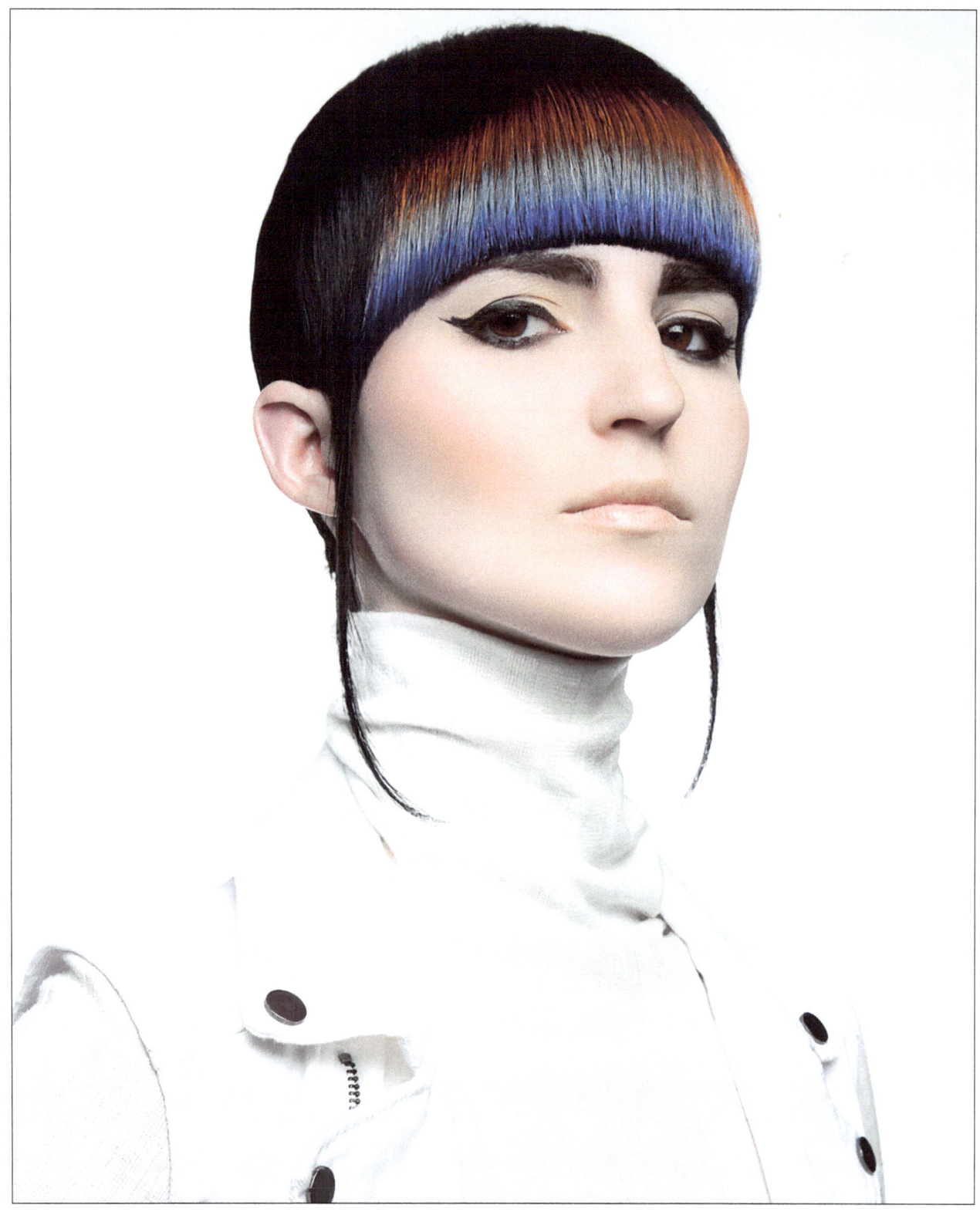

Hair: Dorothy Greene - Make-up: William Molder - Photography: Keith Bryce

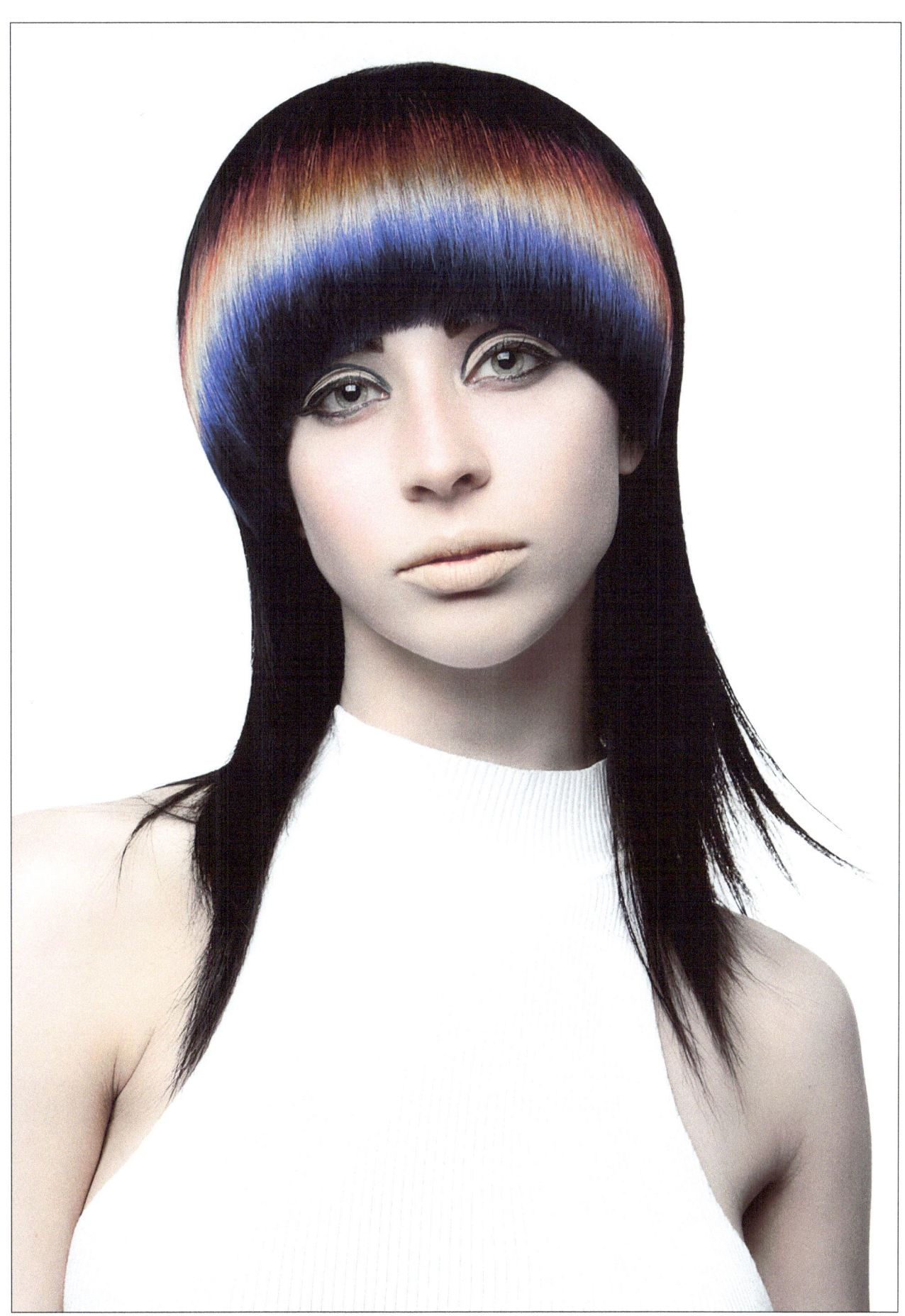

Hair: Dorothy Greene - Make-up: William Molder - Photography: Keith Bryce

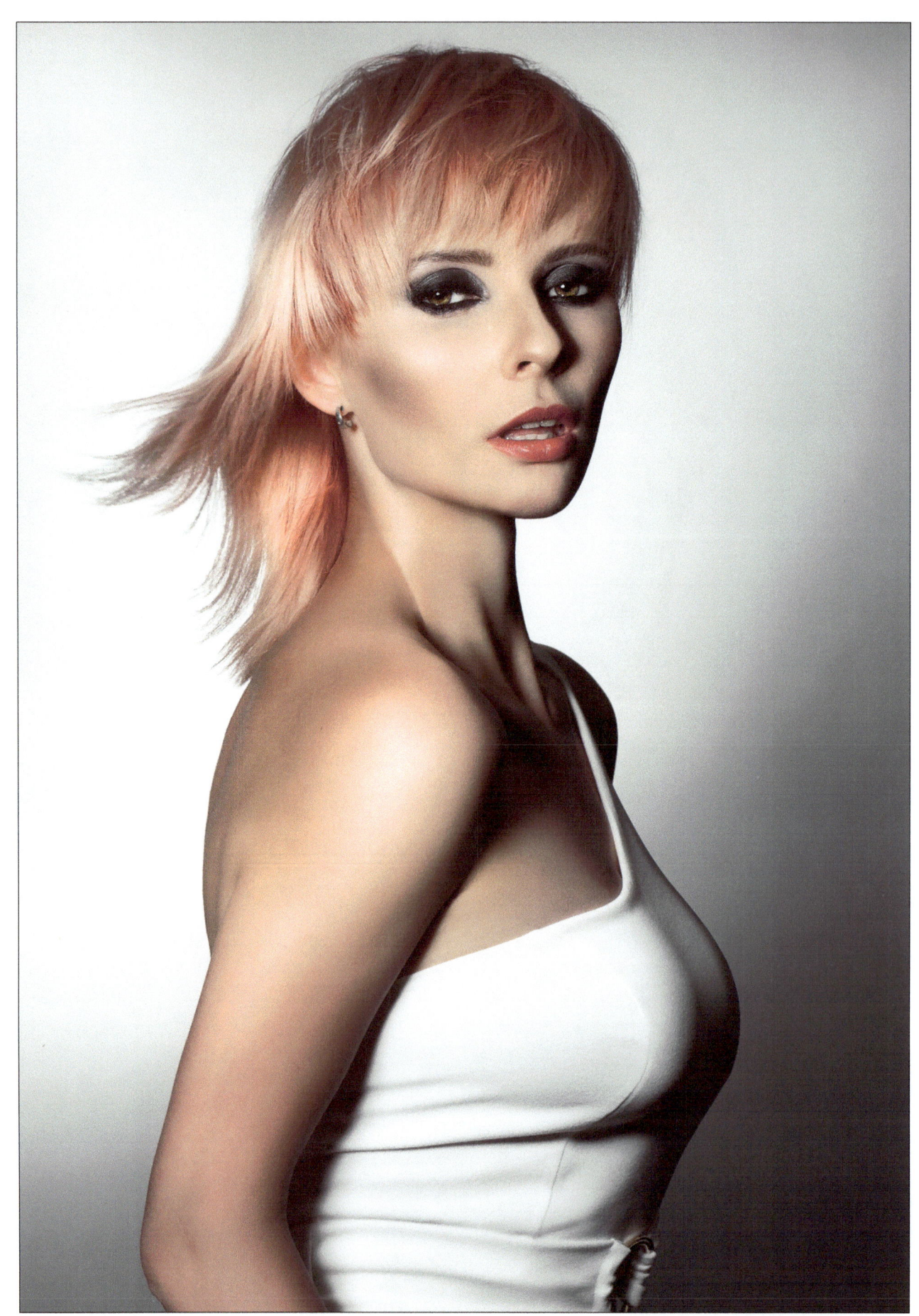

Hair: Ross Charles - Make-up: Sonia Schofield - Styling: Ross Charles - Photography: Ross Charles

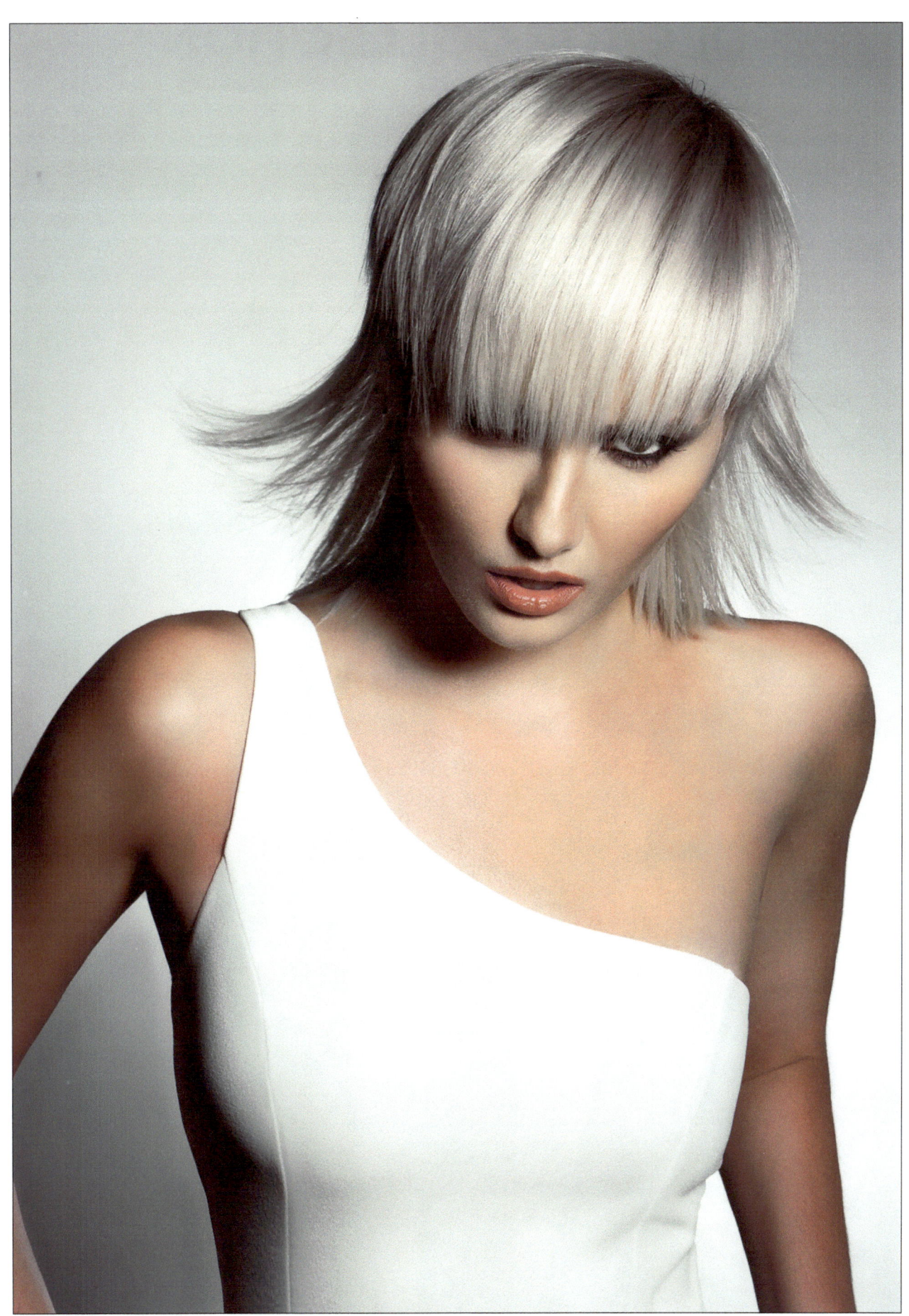

Hair: Ross Charles - Make-up: Sonia Schofield - Styling: Ross Charles - Photography: Ross Charles

DECADE COLLECTION

Jim Shaw, men's hairstyles are forever evolving. Current cuts, including fades and hairstyles shorter at the sides with length on the top, have been extremely popular over the last few years. Recently, quiffs, crops, and smoothly worn precision cuts have topped the charts with an array of mostly polished finishes.

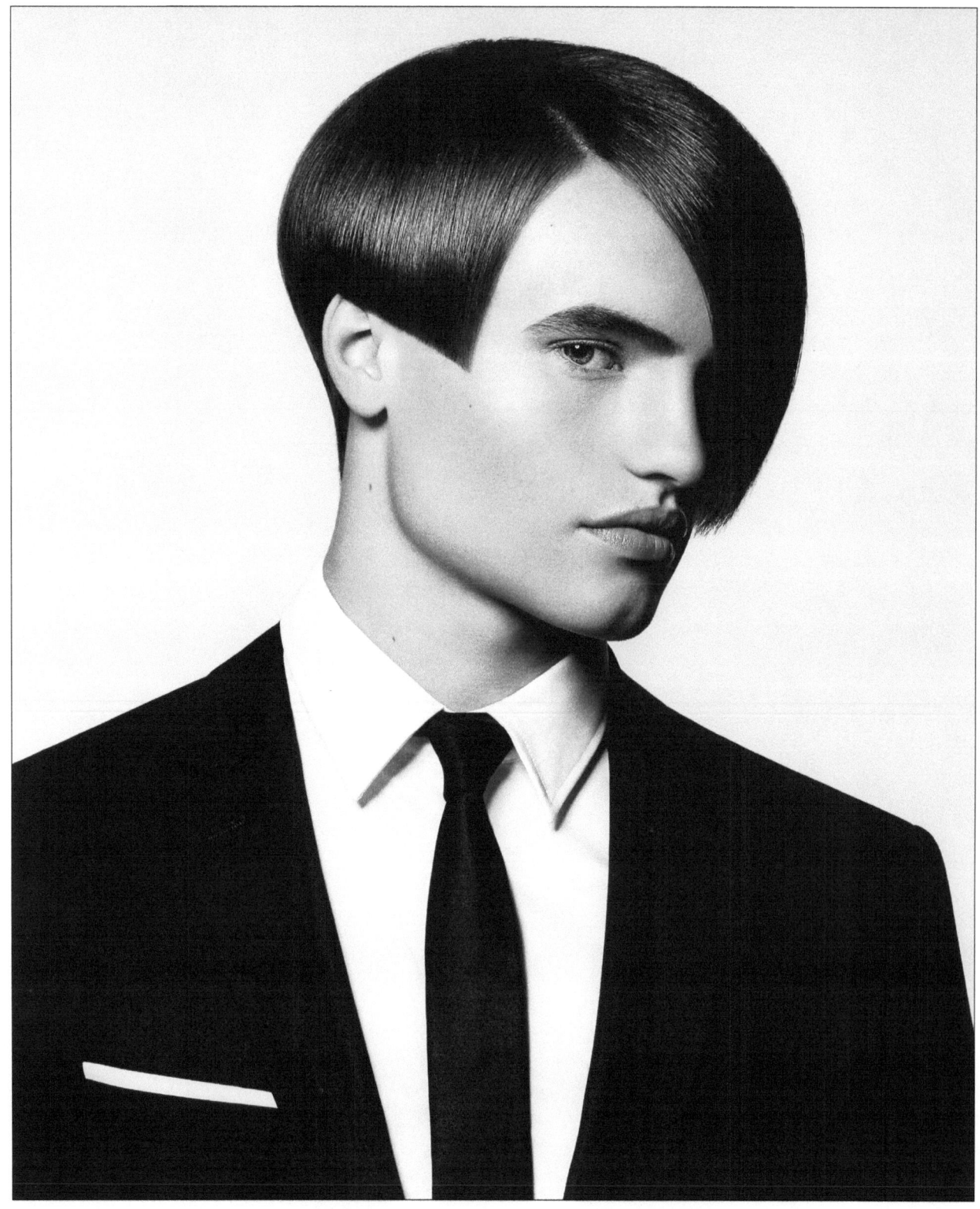

Hair: Jim Shaw - Make-up: Roseanne Velin - Styling: Bernard Connelly - Photography: Tony Le Britton

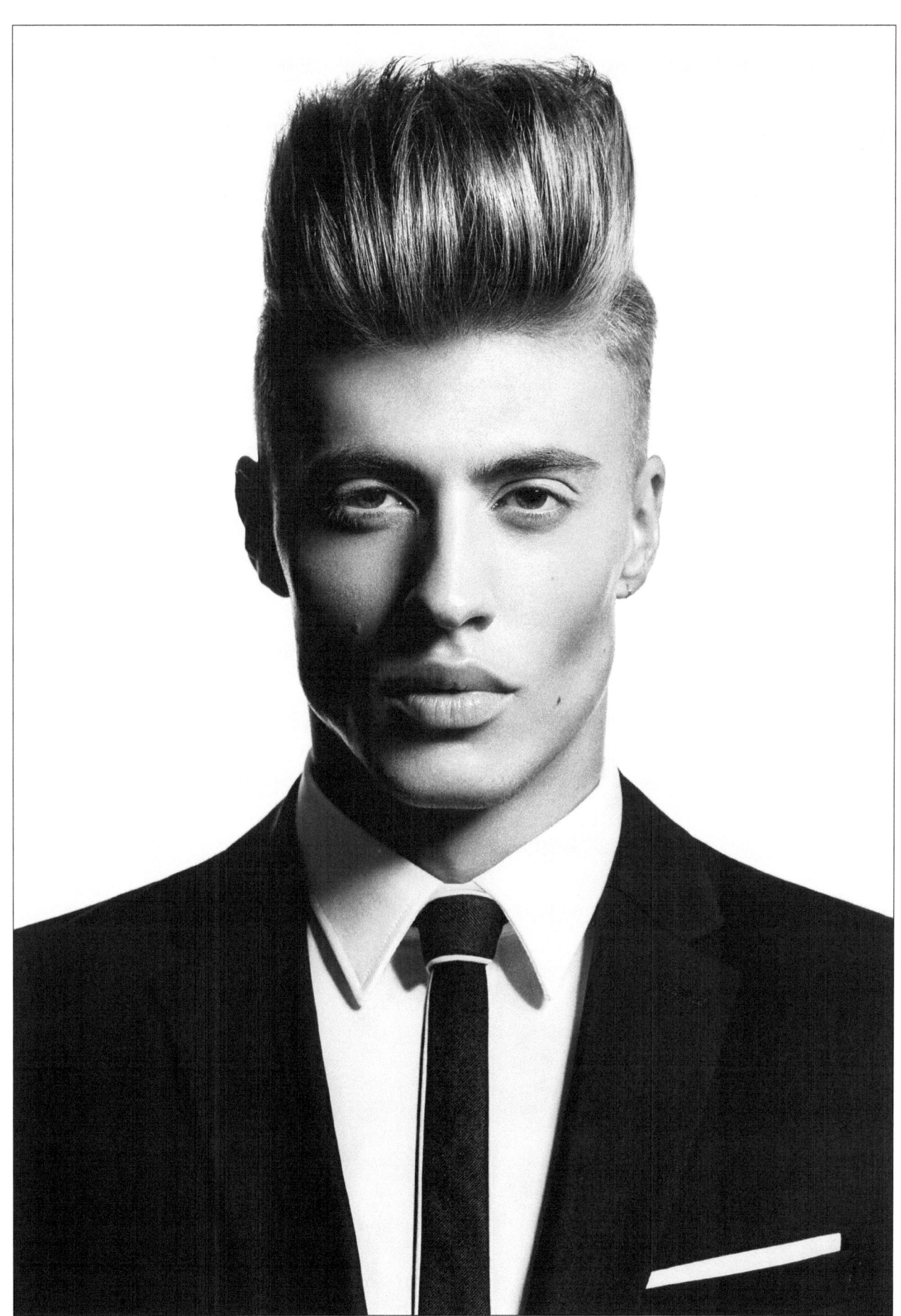

Hair: Jim Shaw - Make-up: Roseanne Velin - Styling: Bernard Connelly - Photography: Tony Le Britton

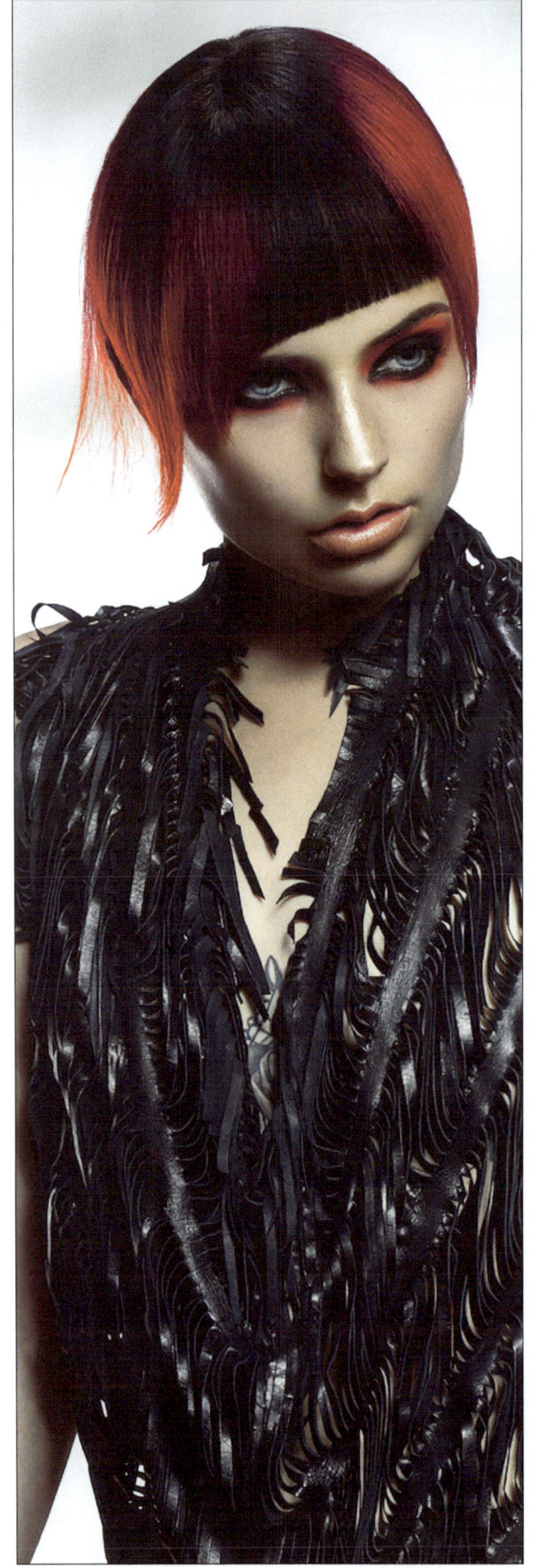
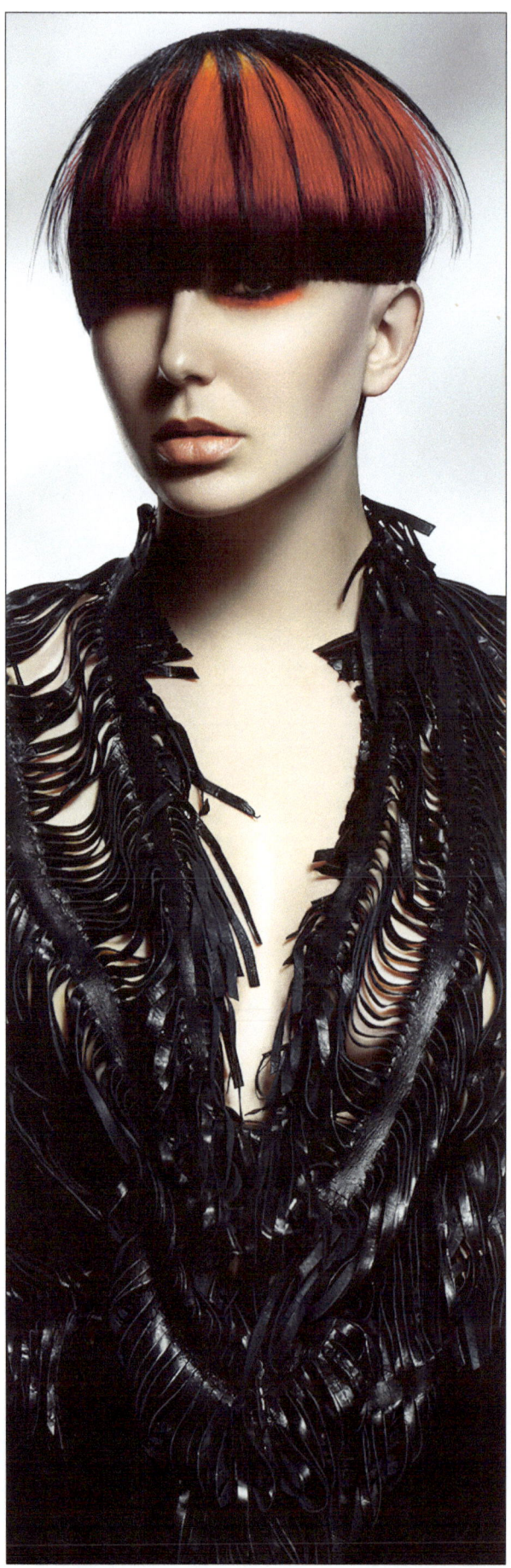

Hair: Chrystofer Benson - Make-up: Danielle Donahue - Photography: John Rawson

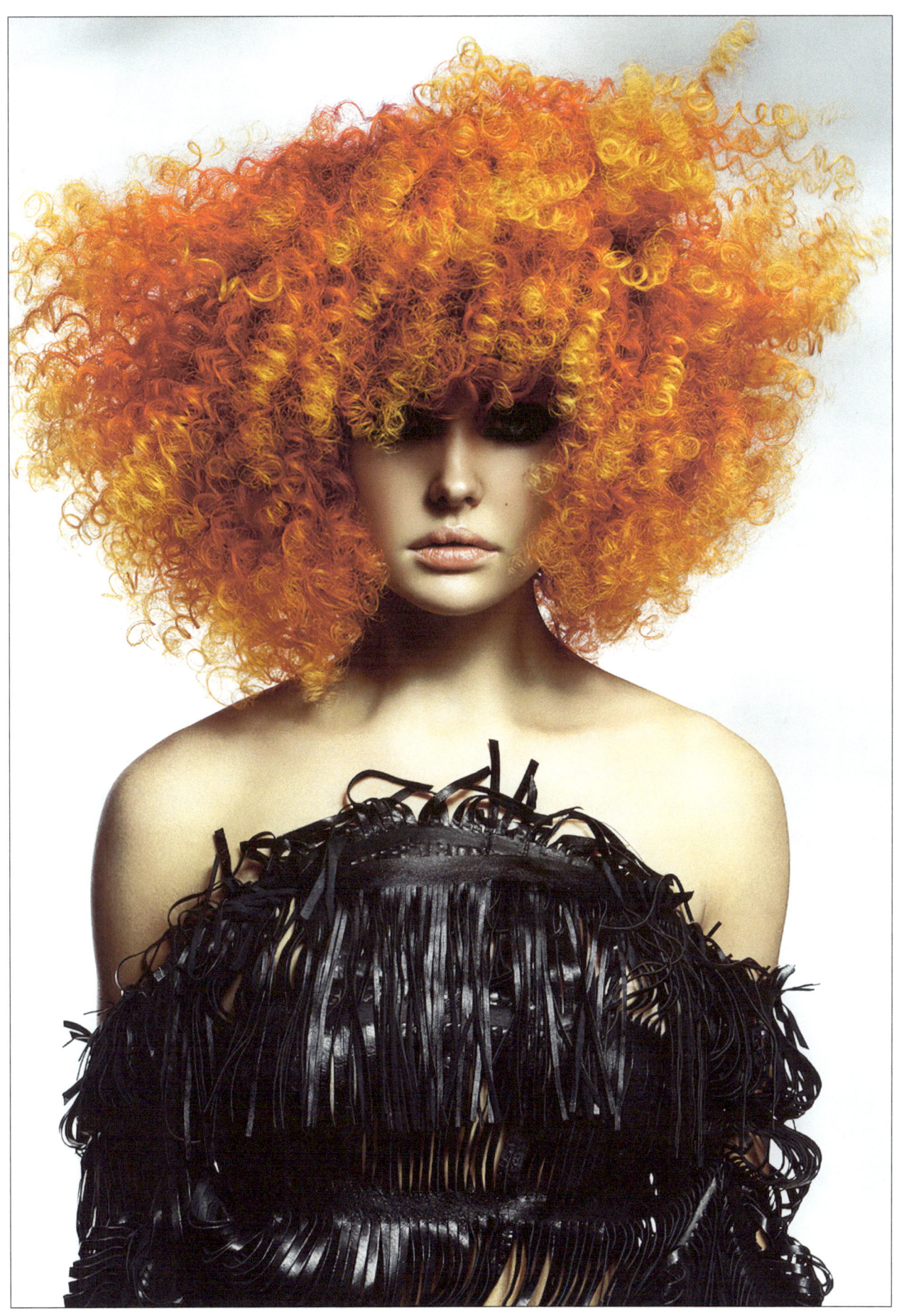

Hair: Chrystofer Benson - Make-up: Danielle Donahue - Photography: John Rawson

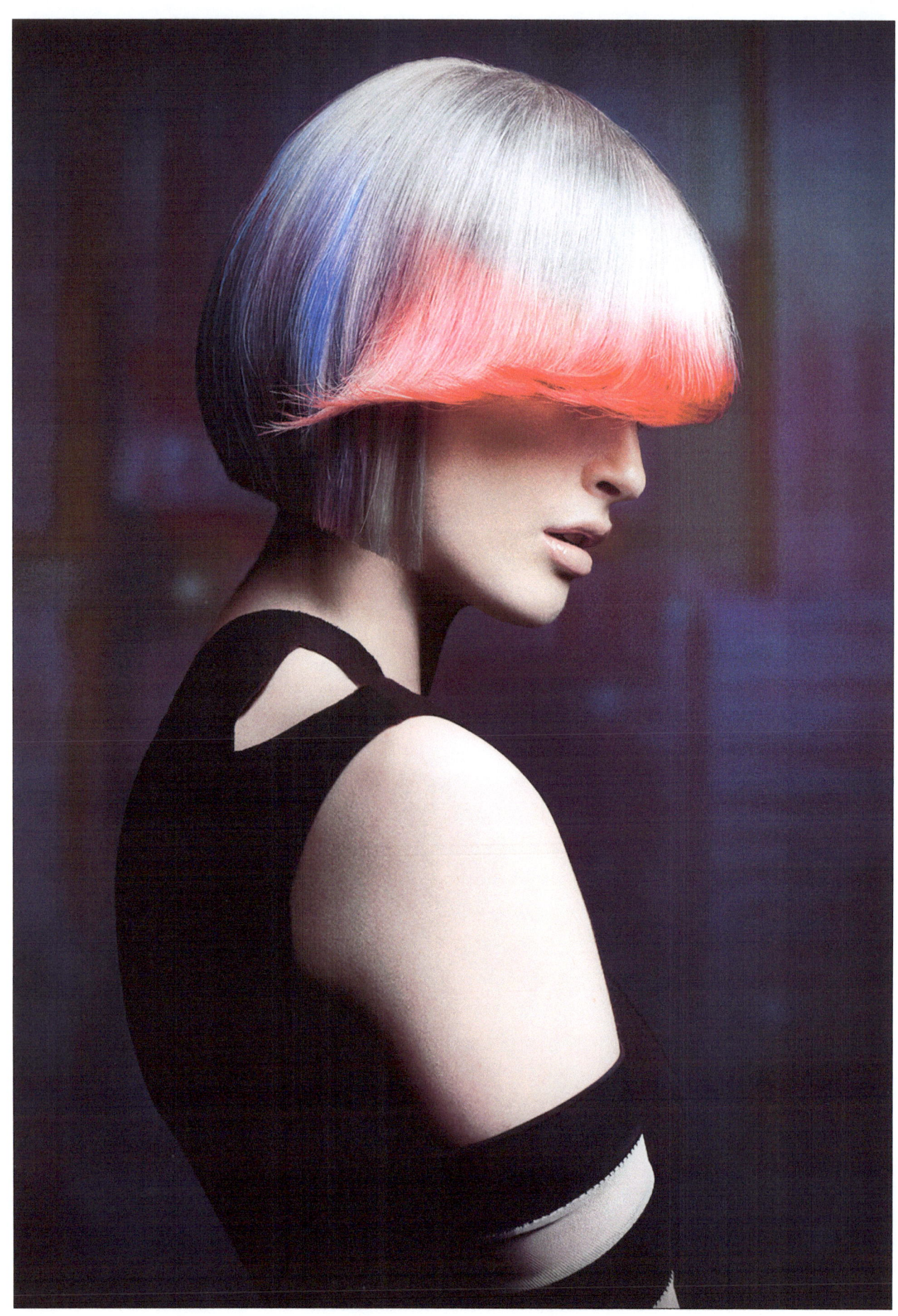

Hair: Ruth Roche - Stiling: Pascal & Jeremie - Make-up: Marie Laure Larrieu & team - Photography: Babak

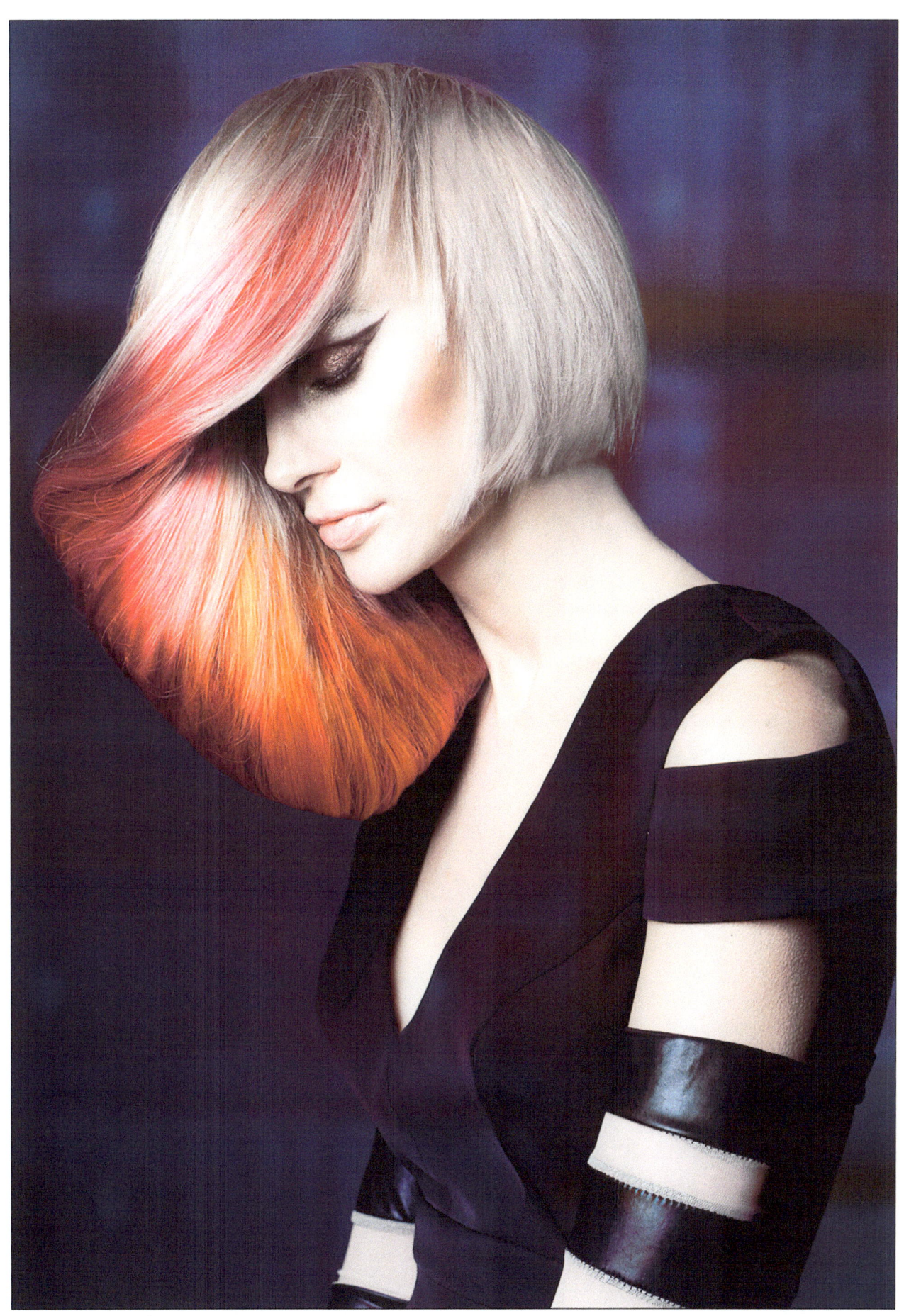

Hair: Ruth Roche - Stiling: Pascal & Jeremie - Make-up: Marie Laure Larrieu & team - Photography: Babak

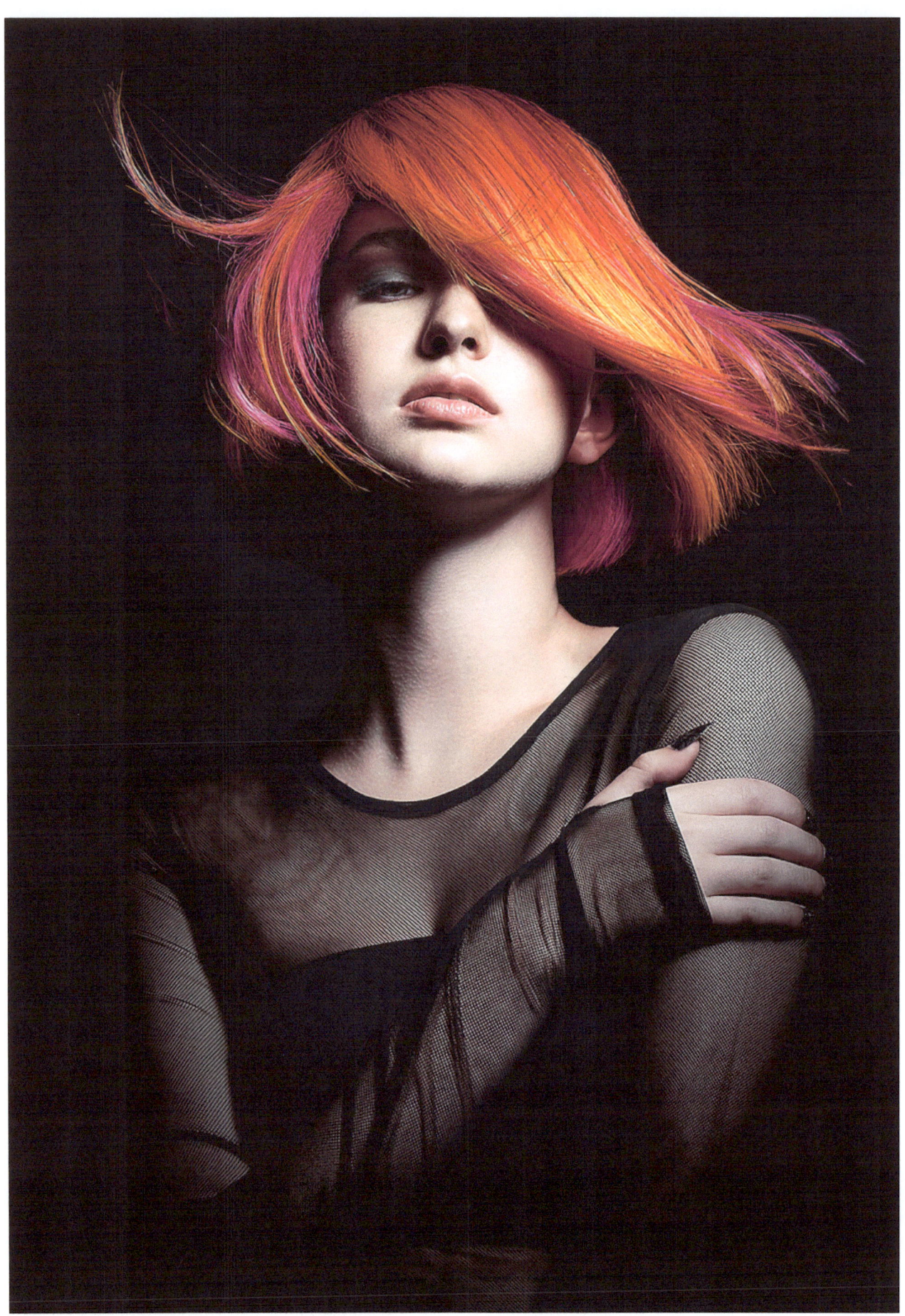

Hair: Allen Ruiz - Make-up: Gabi Hurstado - Photography: Cody Kinsfather

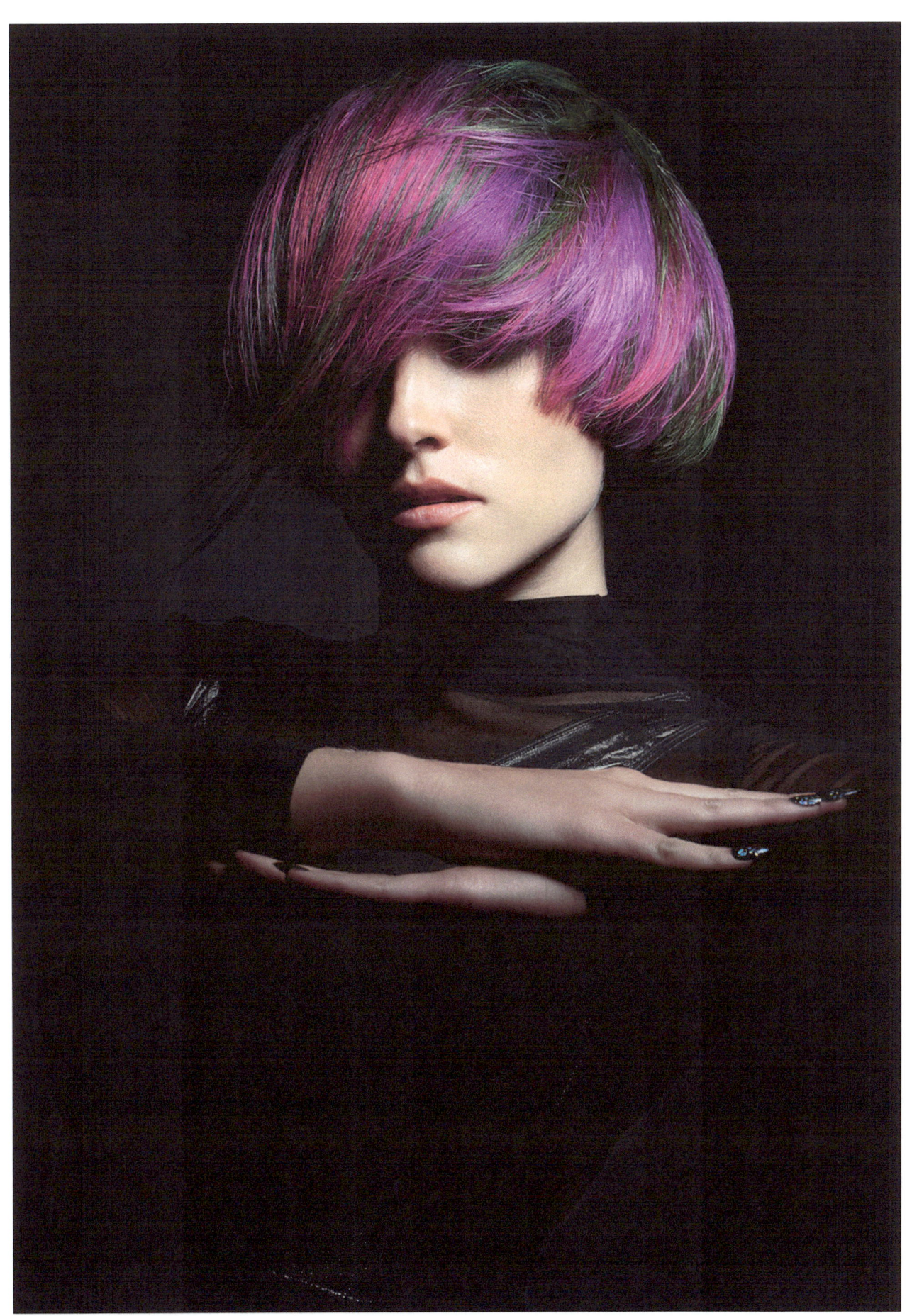

Hair: Allen Ruiz - Make-up: Gabi Hurstado - Photography: Cody Kinsfather

COLOR INSPIRATION

#truestory there is one salon brand that has 2020 written all over it; Marc Antoni is a family business with heart and hell-raising in equal measure and talented colourist Dan Spiller is a part of it too. We've spotted that ever since 'Dad' Bruno Giamettei opened up shop in 1966, his philosophy of loving clients.

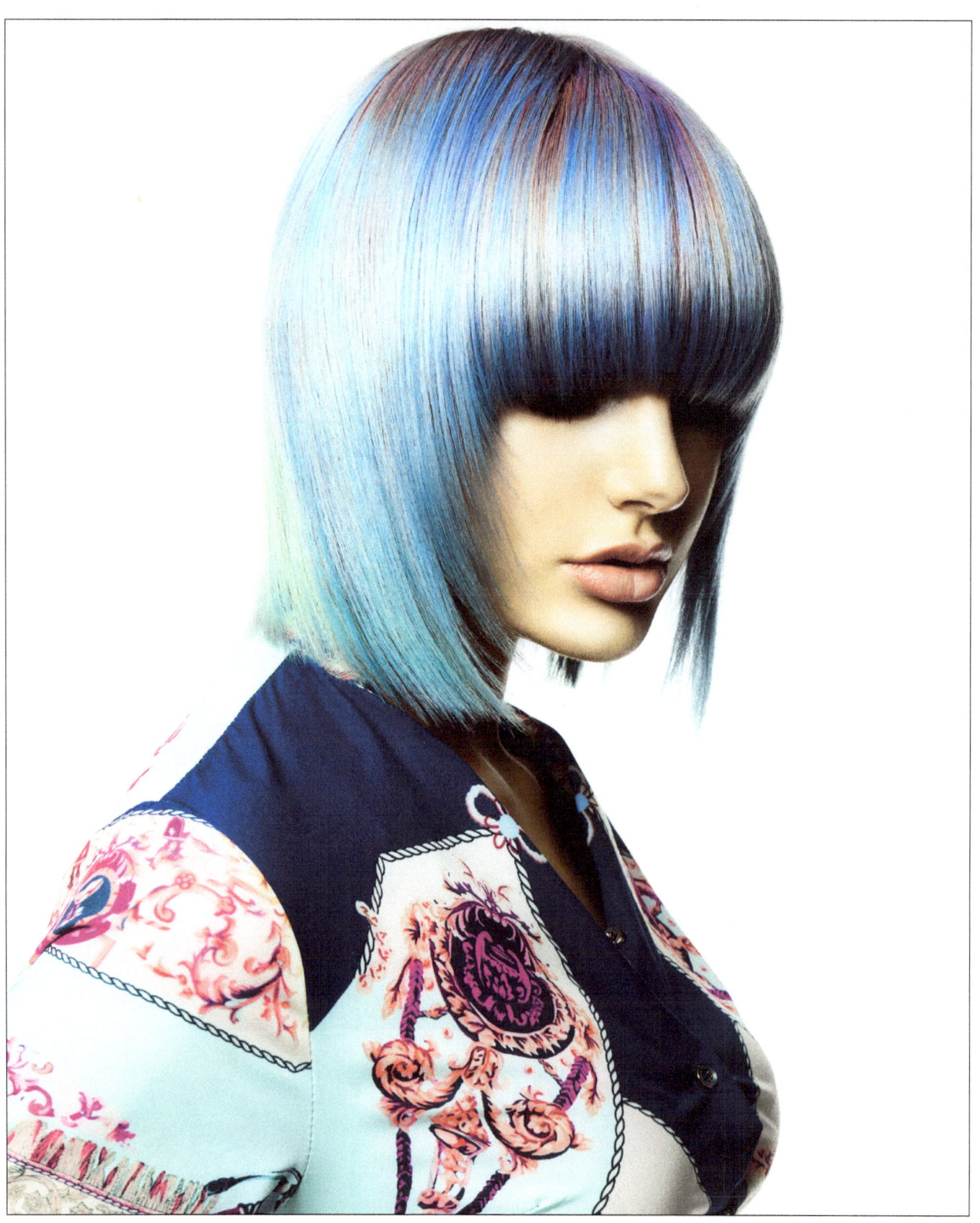

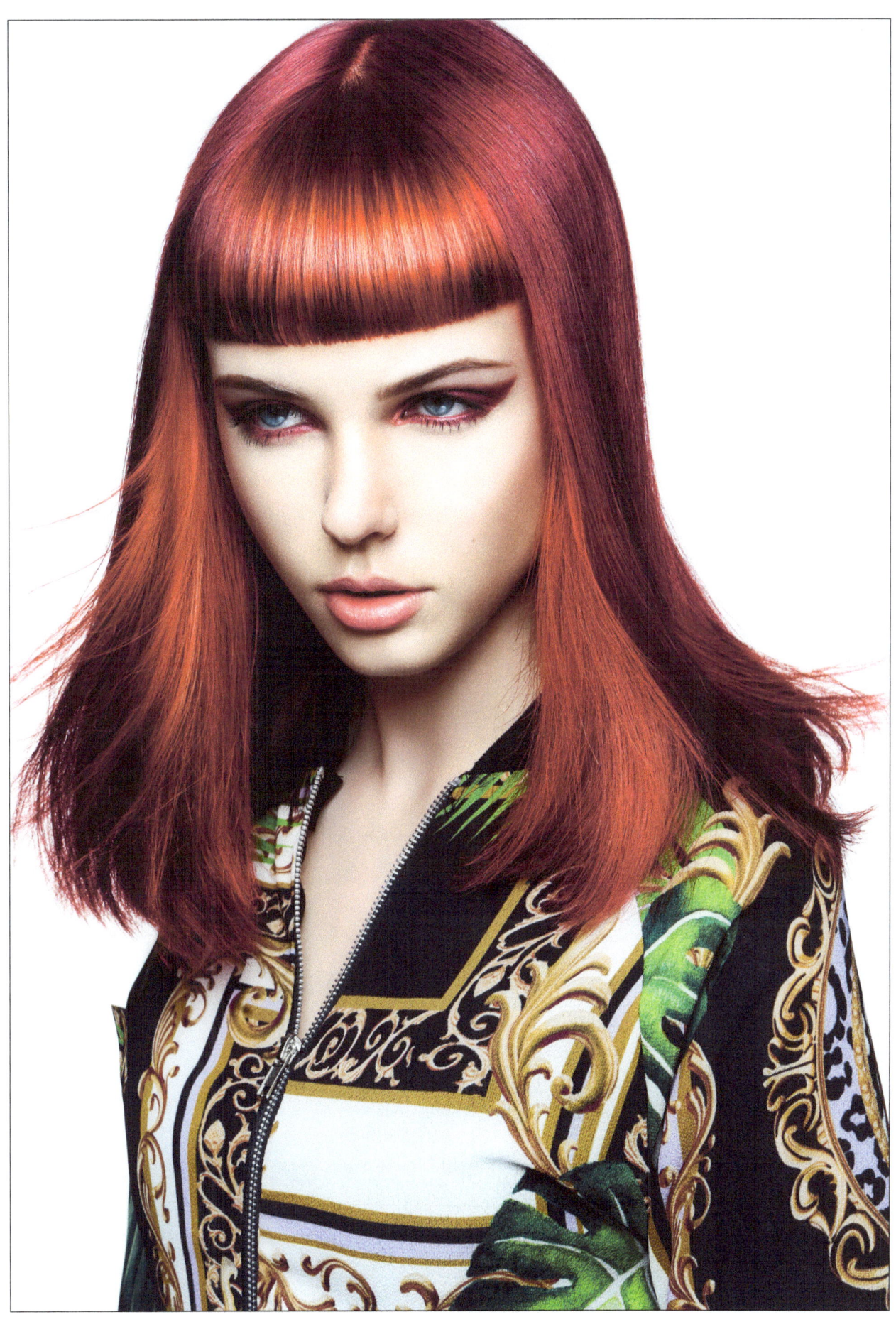

Hair: Dan Spiller for Marc Antoni - Make-up: Katie Moore - Styling: Bruno Marc - Photography: Jamie Blanchard

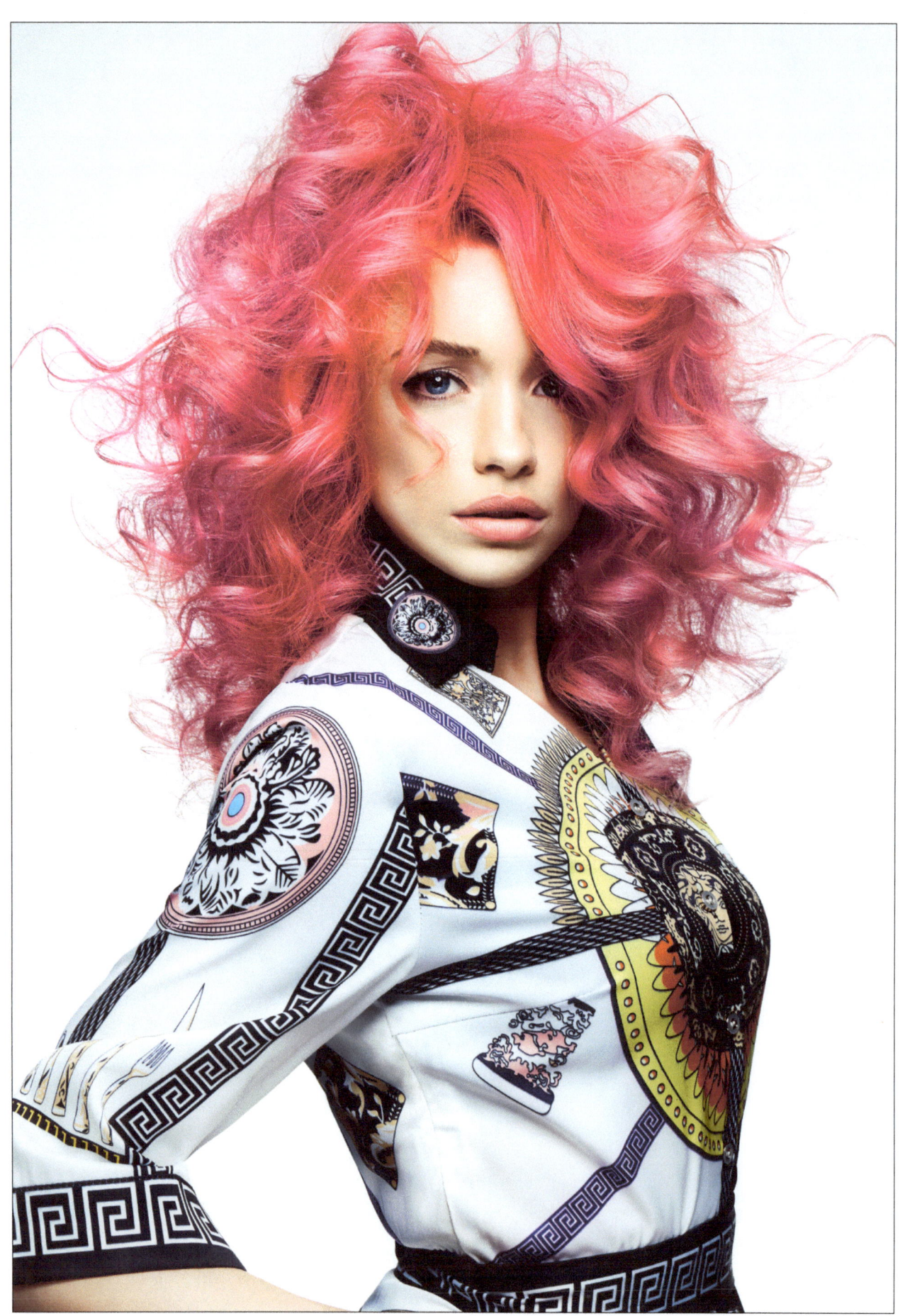

Hair: Dan Spiller for Marc Antoni - Make-up: Katie Moore - Styling: Bruno Marc - Photography: Jamie Blanchard

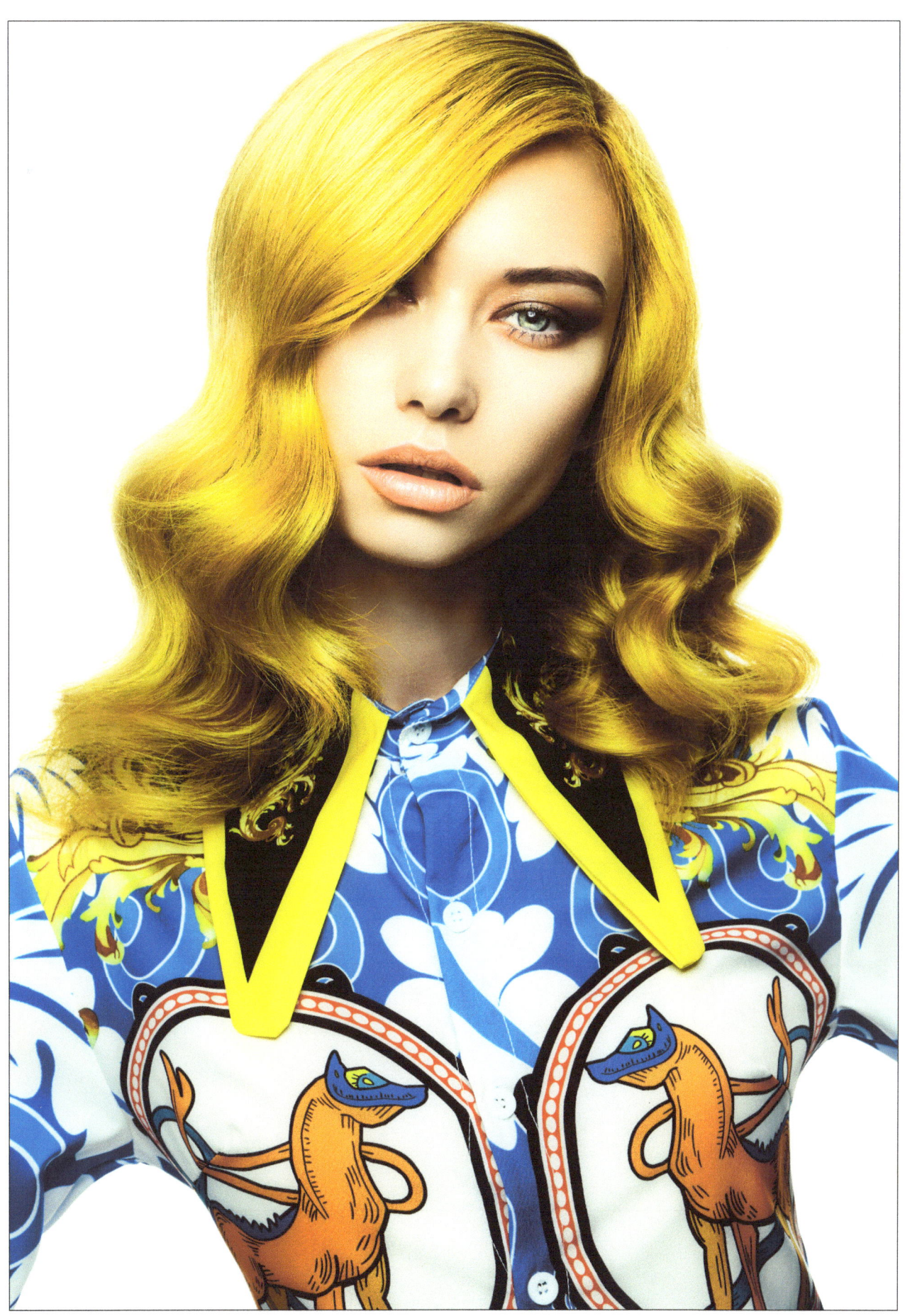

Hair: Dan Spiller for Marc Antoni - Make-up: Katie Moore - Styling: Bruno Marc - Photography: Jamie Blanchard

LINEAR COLLECTION

In this collection the diverse styles show a multitude of skill and technique. The collection celebrates classic and contemporary men's hairdressing, with the styling and lighting used creating a real emphasis on the hair.

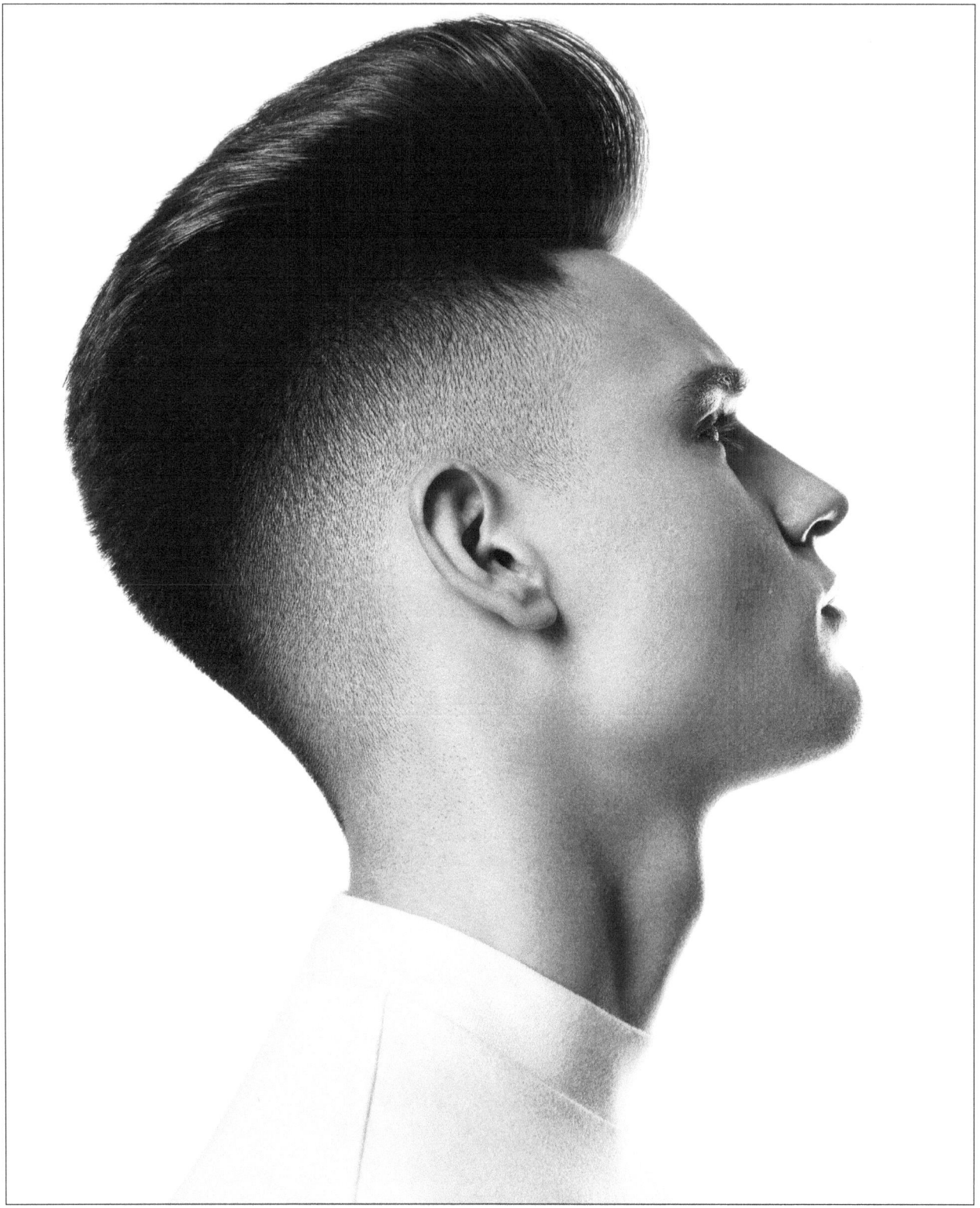

Hair: Jim Shaw and Daisy Carter - Make-up: Roseanna Velin - Styling: Jim Shaw - Photography: Tony Le Britton

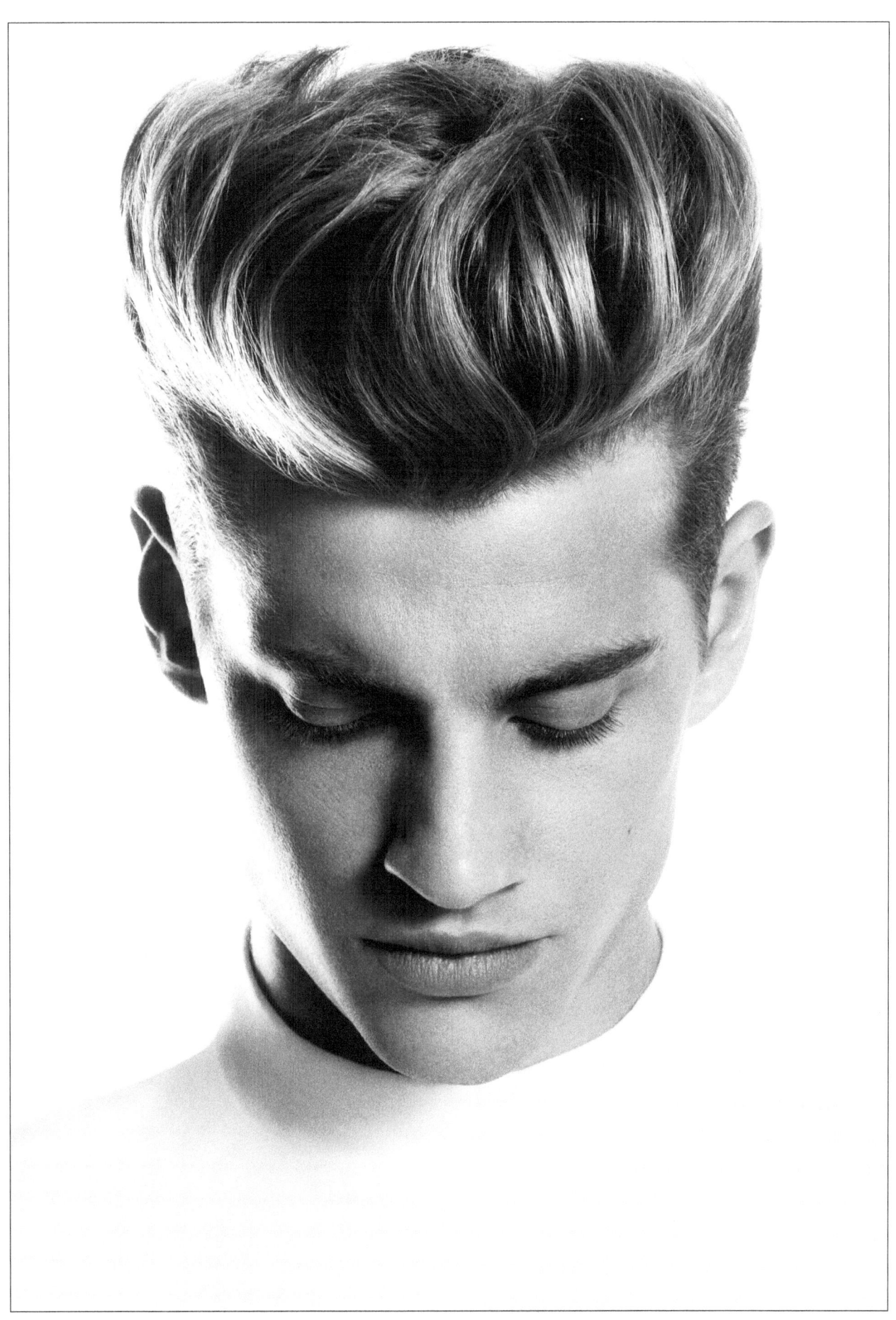

Hair: Jim Shaw and Daisy Carter - Make-up: Roseanna Velin - Styling: Jim Shaw - Photography: Tony Le Britton

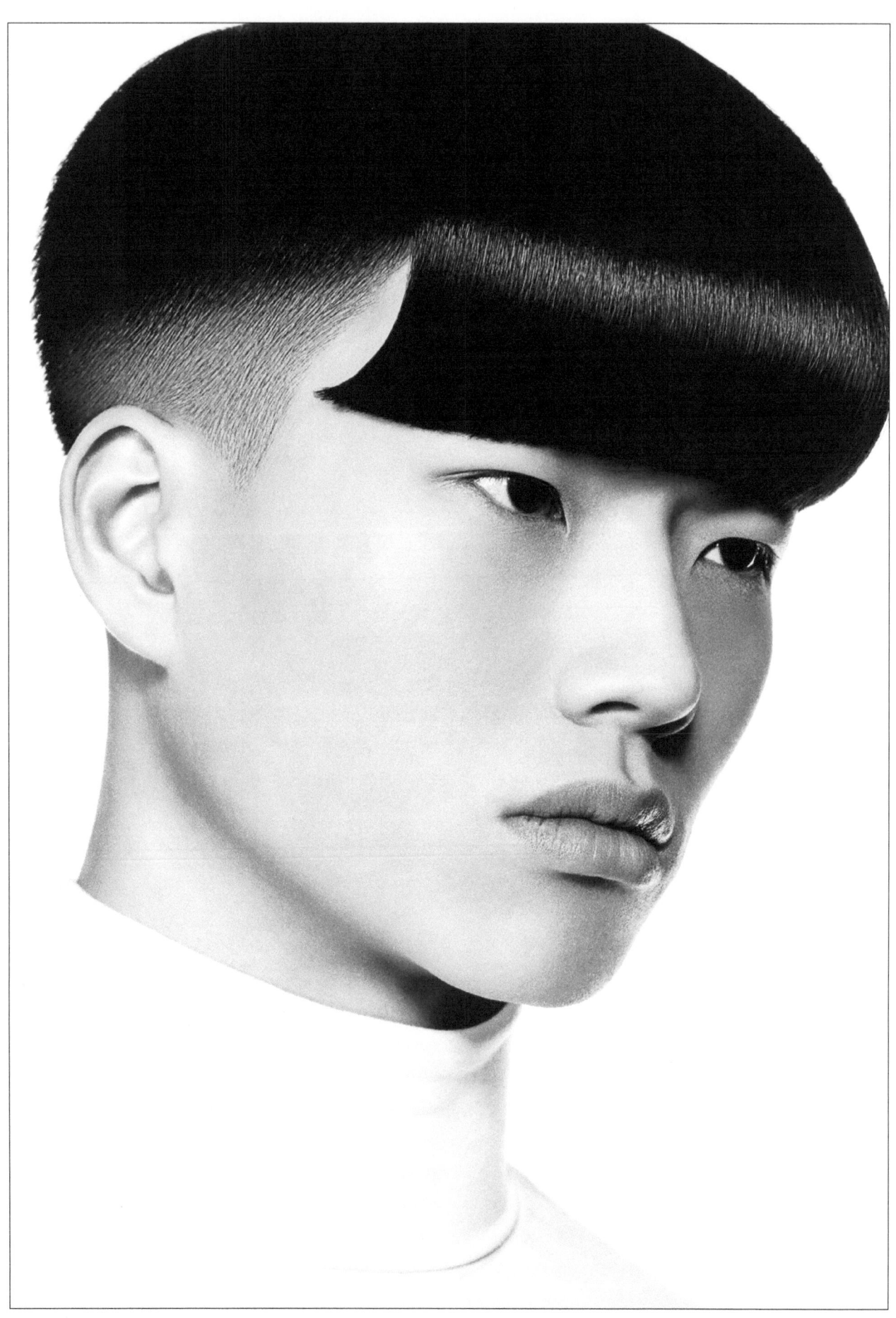

Hair: Jim Shaw and Daisy Carter - Make-up: Roseanna Velin - Styling: Jim Shaw - Photography: Tony Le Britton

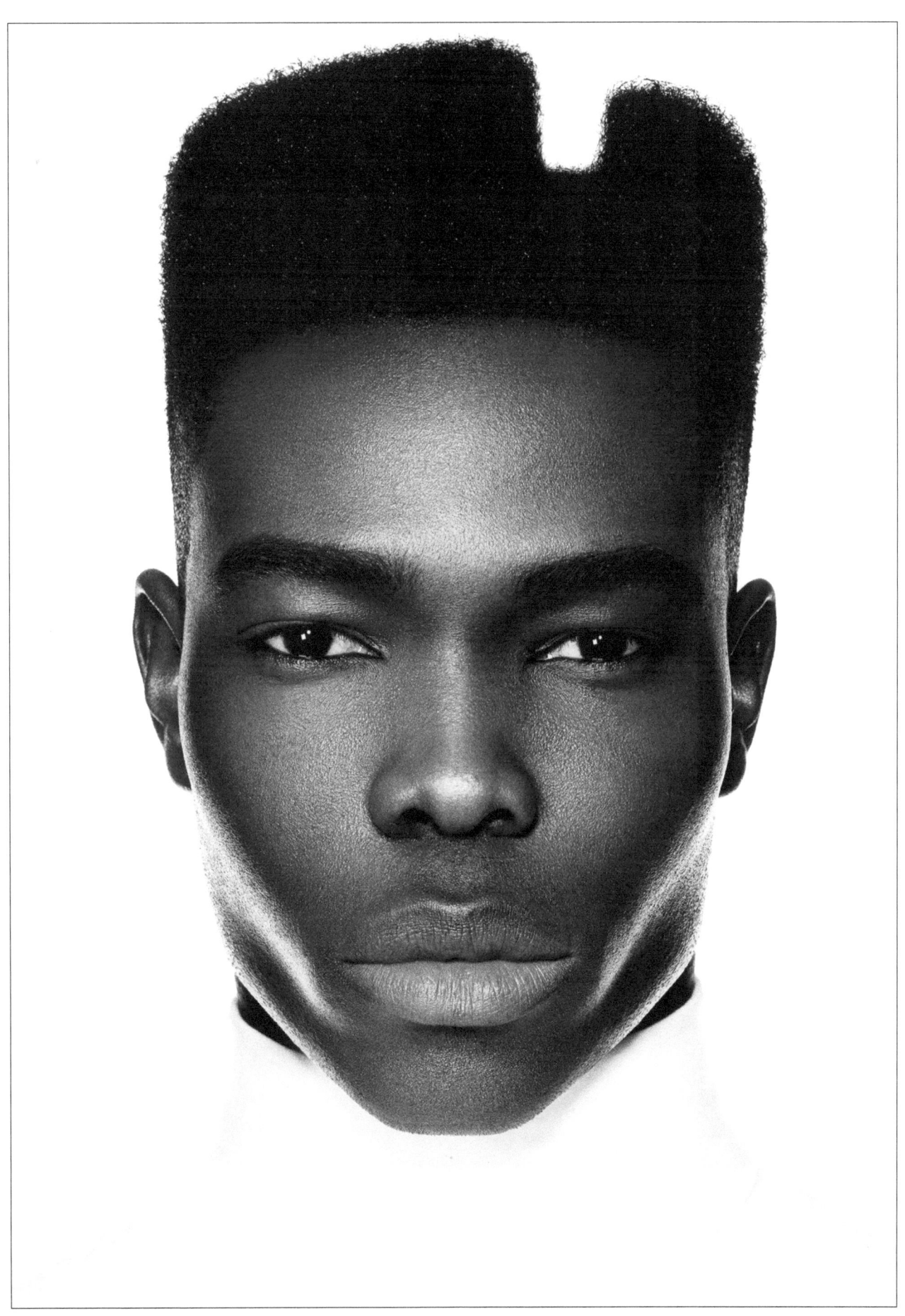

Hair: Jim Shaw and Daisy Carter - Make-up: Roseanna Velin - Styling: Jim Shaw - Photography: Tony Le Britton

CLASH COLLECTION

New and exciting Mark Leeson spring-summer 2020 collection that delivers dynamic British youthfulness. It fuses color and cut together utilizing modern techniques that evoke desirable yet wearable hair. High-end luxury fashion creates an up-tempo clash of the bold, identifiable vibrancy of color, print, and texture.

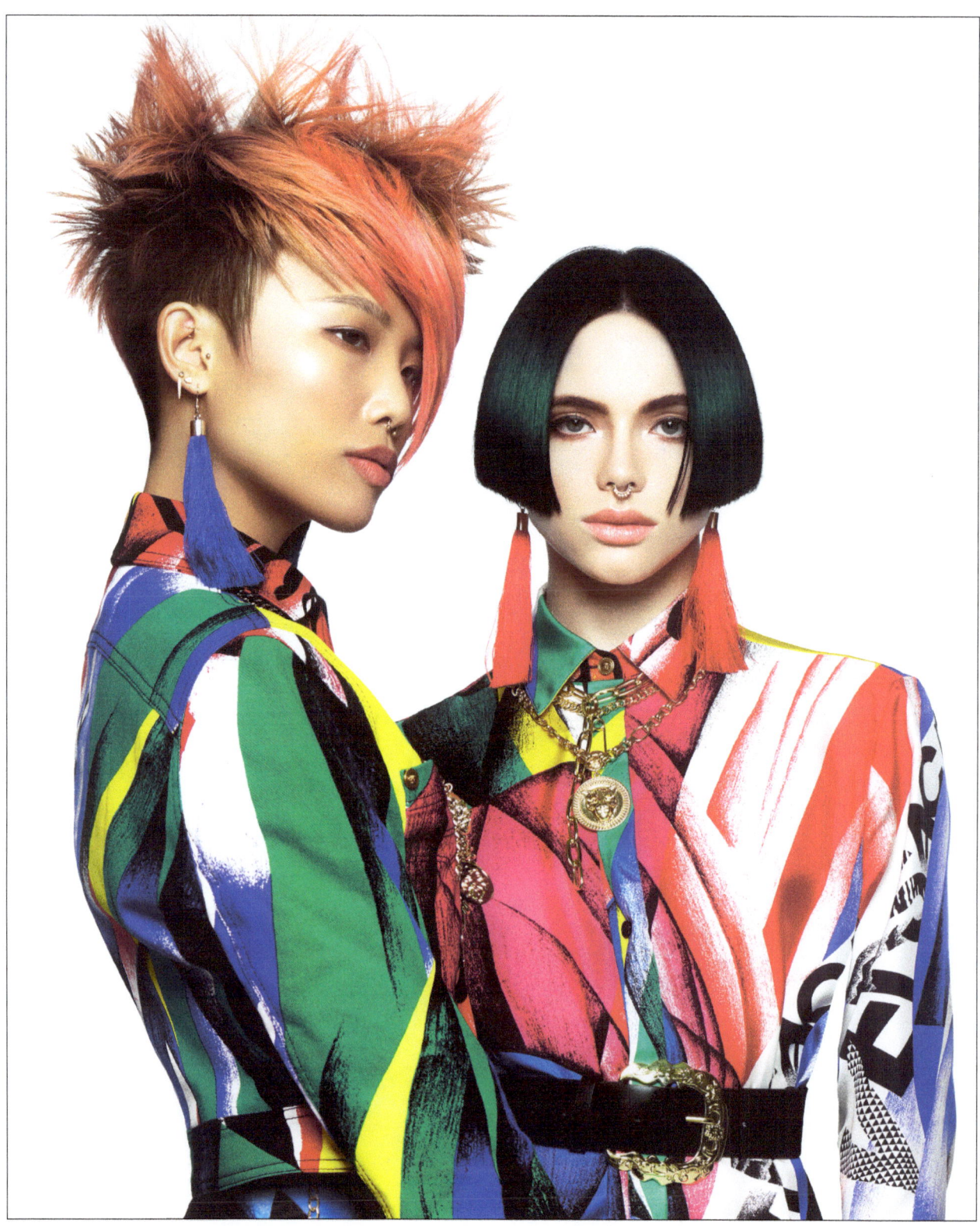

Hair: Mark Leeson - Make-up: Lan Nyguen Grais - Styling: M&R - Photography: Richard Miles

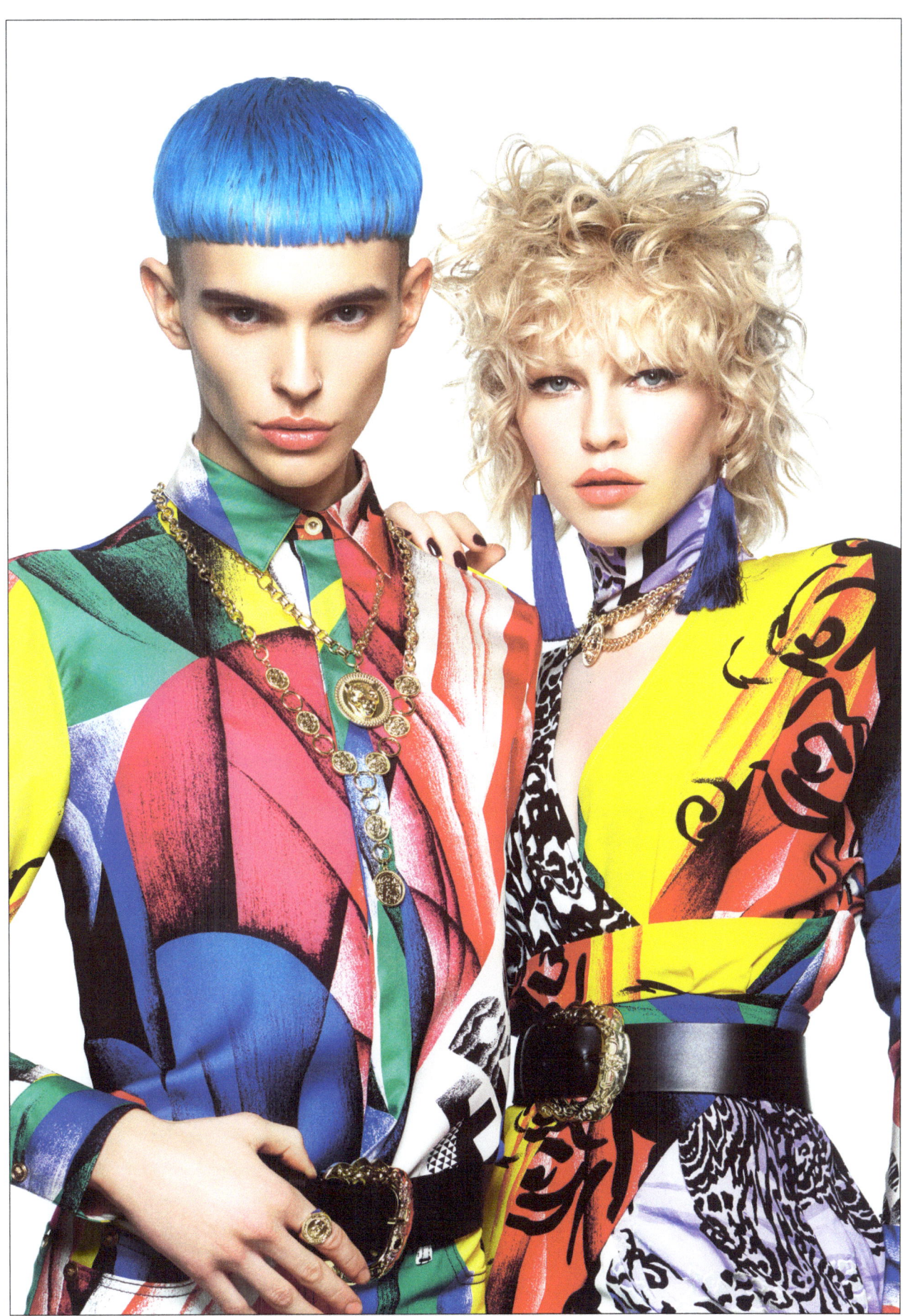

Hair: Mark Leeson - Make-up: Lan Nyguen Grais - Styling: M&R - Photography: Richard Miles

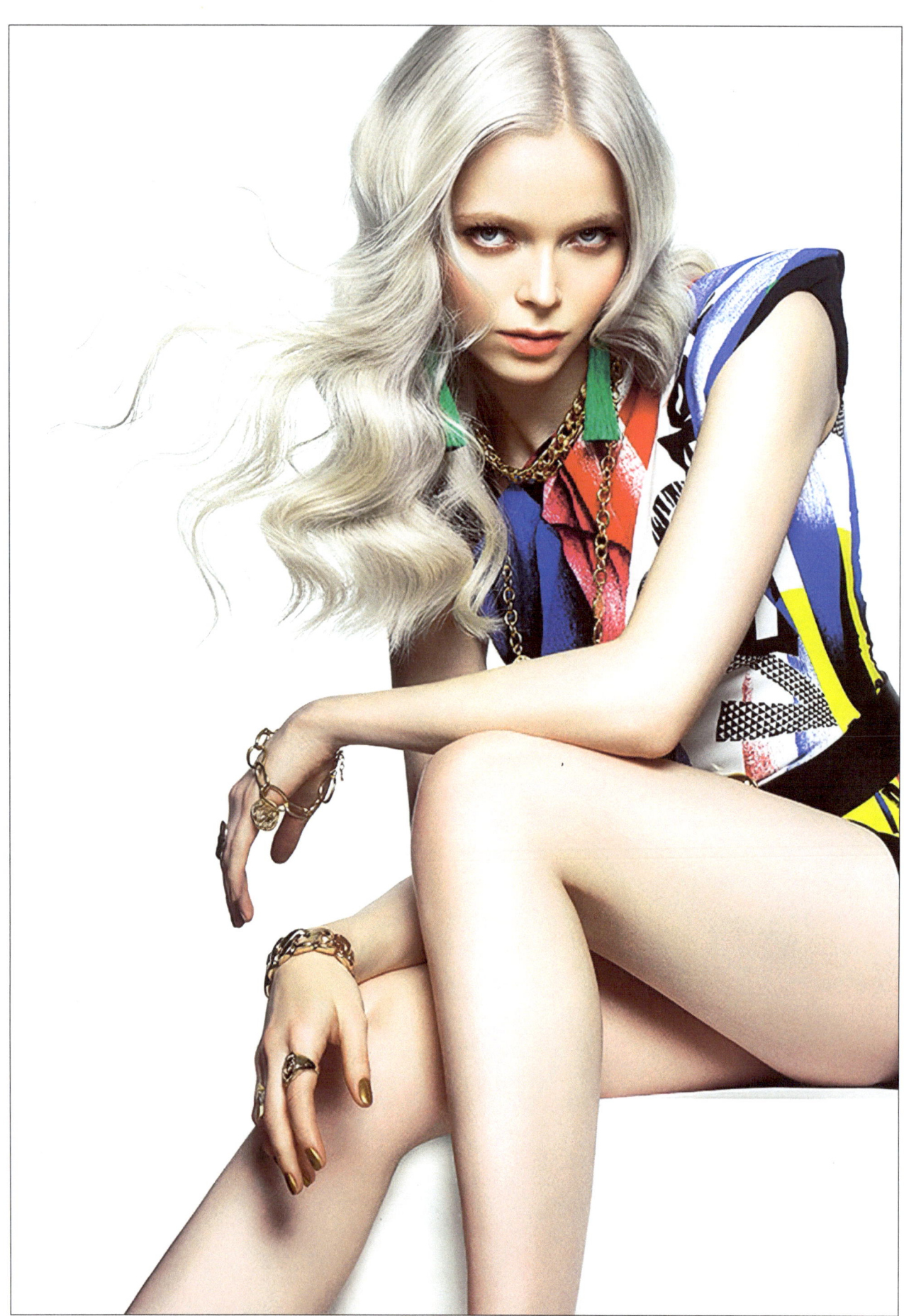

Hair: Mark Leeson - Make-up: Lan Nyguen Grais - Styling: M&R - Photography: Richard Miles

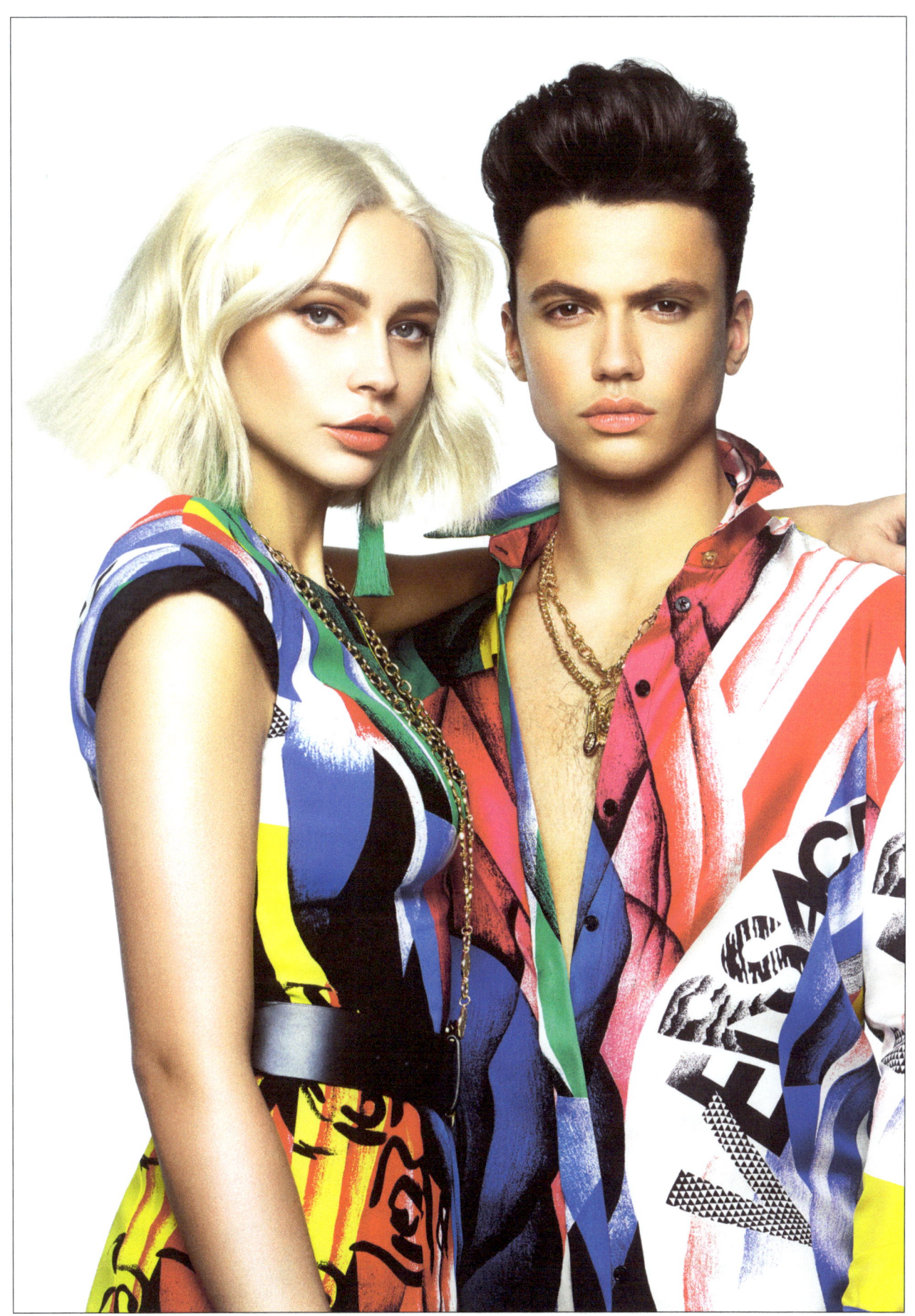

Hair: Mark Leeson - Make-up: Lan Nyguen Grais - Styling: M&R - Photography: Richard Miles

PRIVÉ COLLECTION

This incredible new colour collection shows off the team's skills perfectly, with the infusion of many colours and techniques used to create these wonderful images.

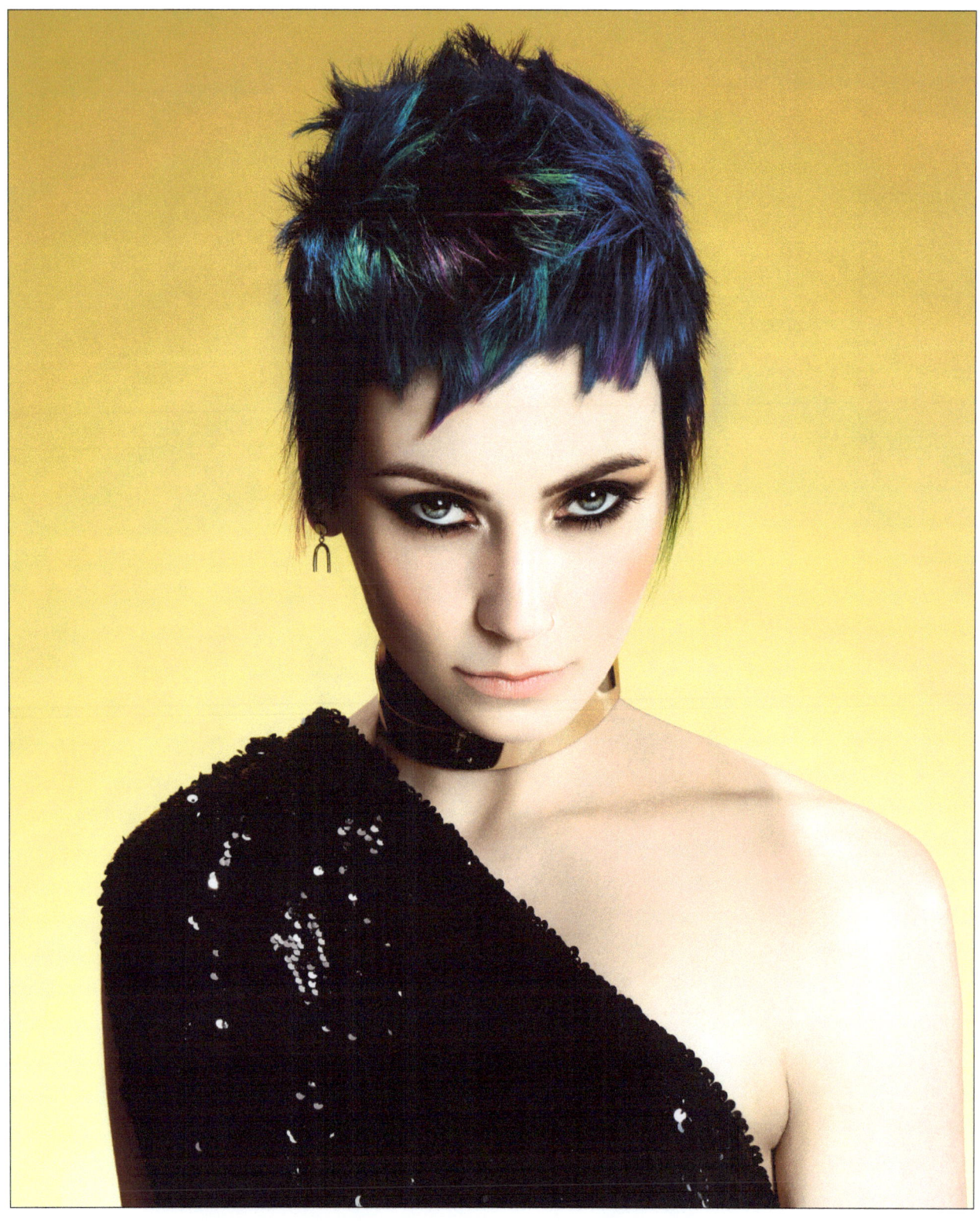

Hair: Rainbow Room International Artistic Team - Make-up: Lan Nguyen-Grealis - Styling: Jamie Russel - Photography: John Rawson

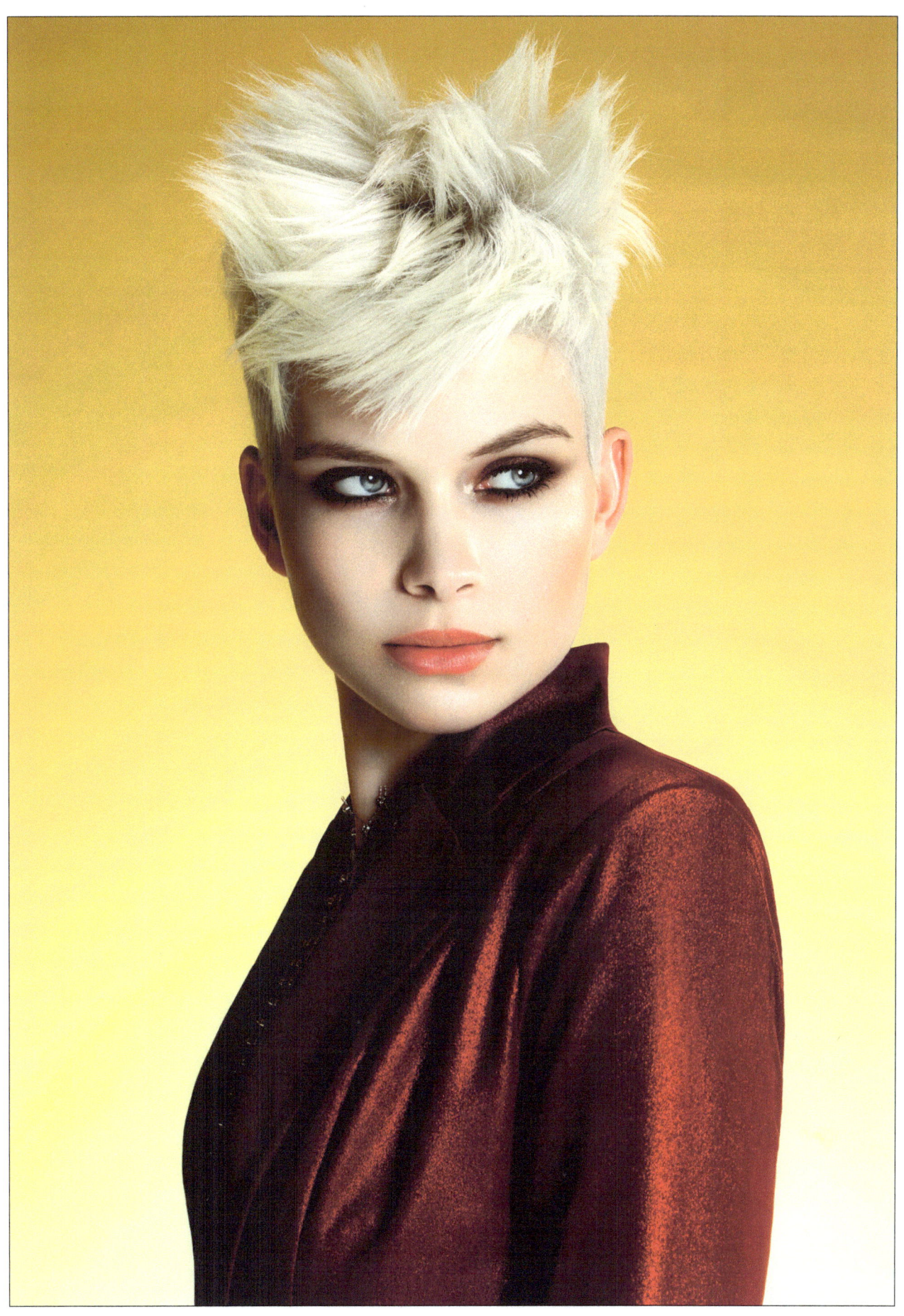

Hair: Rainbow Room International Artistic Team - Make-up: Lan Nguyen-Grealis - Styling: Jamie Russel - Photography: John Rawson

HAIR @ 58

A new collection from Sam Bell @ Hair At 58 explores the trend for putting two models in a photograph and showcasing the drama of diametrically opposed styles. Curls, fringes, textures and volume are explored in striking imagery (shot gorgeously by Tony Le Britton.

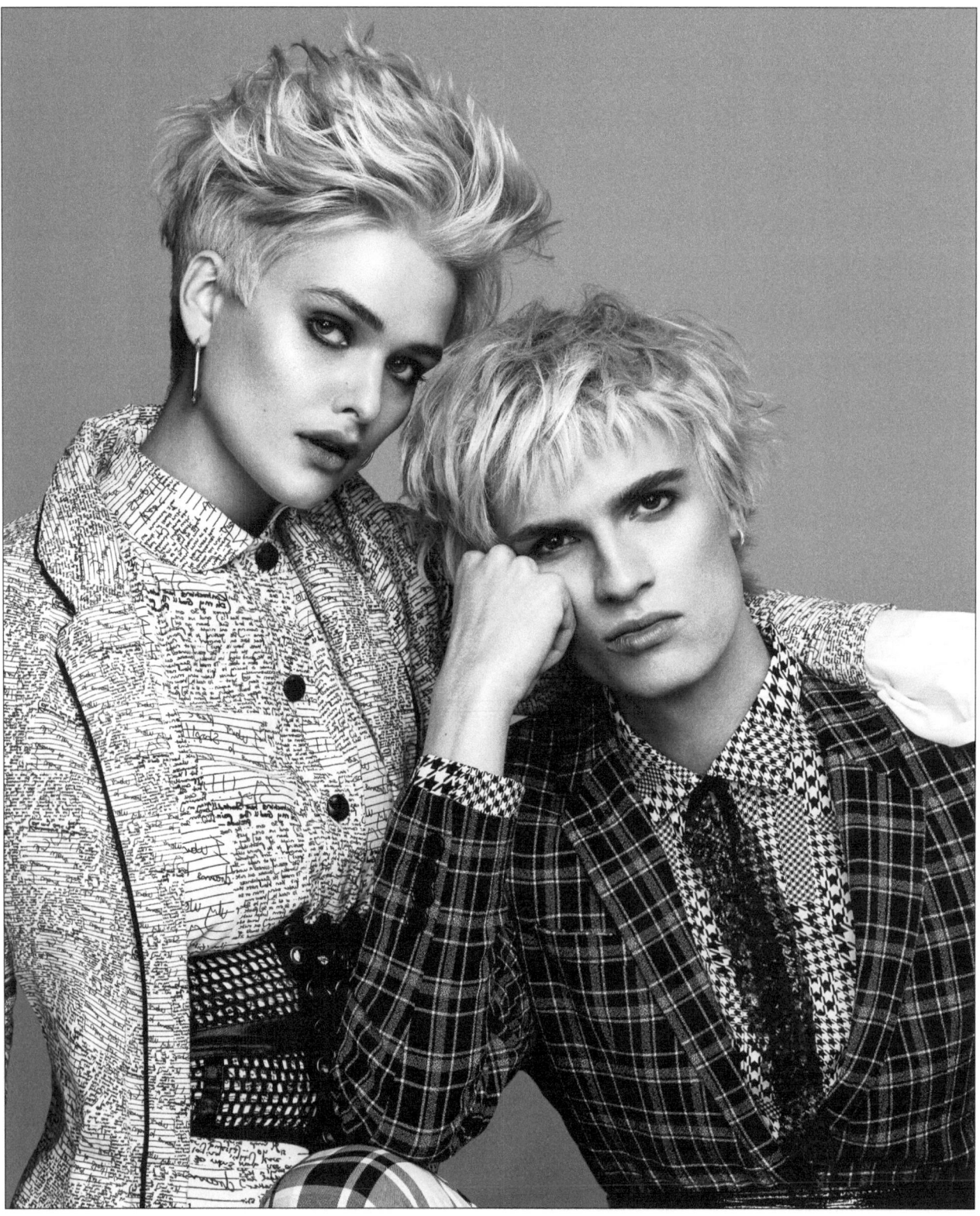

Hair: Sam Bell, Hair At 58 - Make-up: Roseanna Veline Britton - Styling: Joey Bevan - Photography: Tony Le Britton

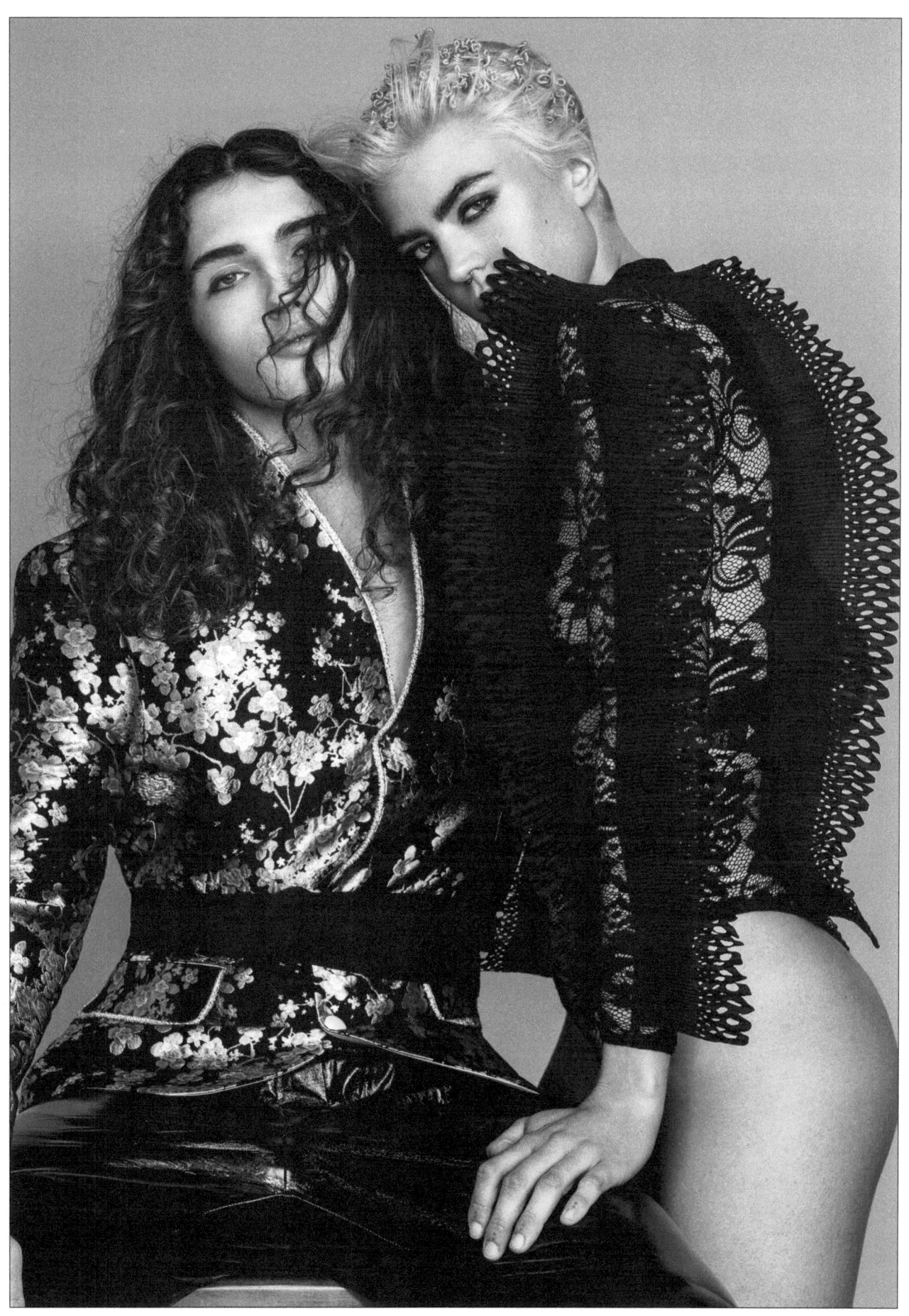

Hair: Sam Bell, Hair At 58 - Make-up: Roseanna Veline Britton - Styling: Joey Bevan - Photography: Tony Le Britton

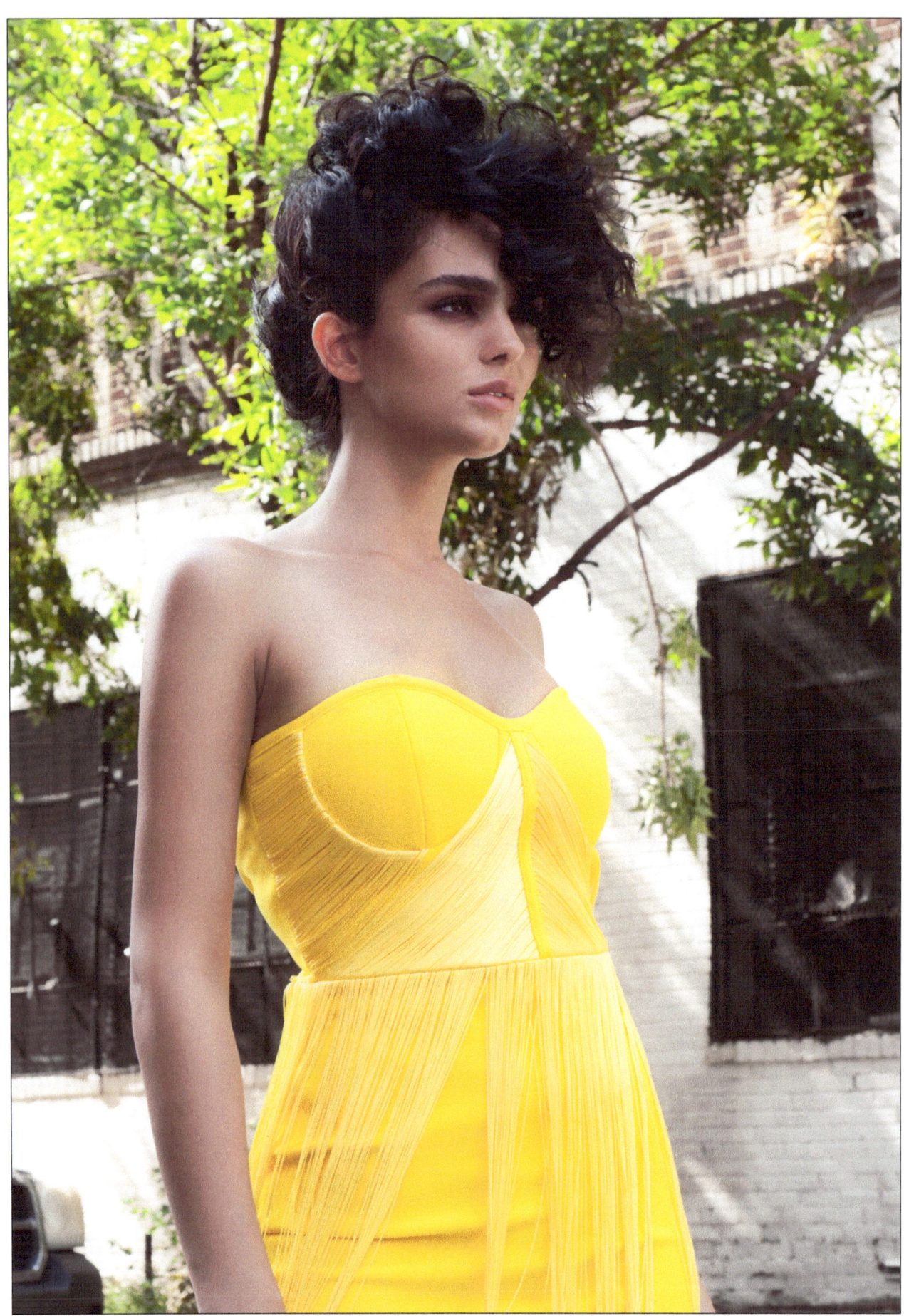

Hair: Neil Smith & Mirza Batanovic - Make-up: Emilia Adamkiewicz - Styling: Destiny Waldon - Photography: Mark Short

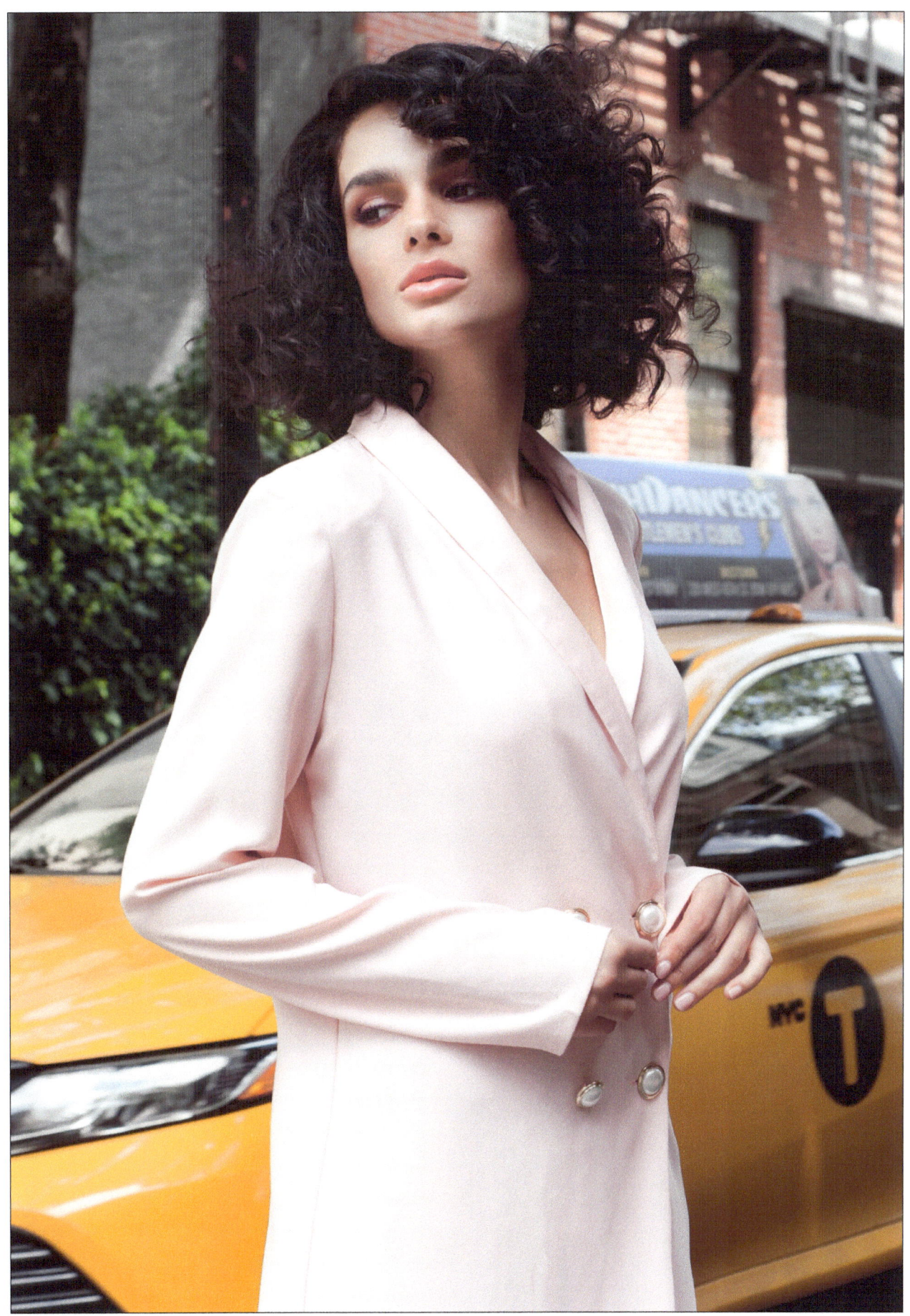

Hair: Neil Smith & Mirza Batanovic - Make-up: Emilia Adamkiewicz - Styling: Destiny Waldon - Photography: Mark Short

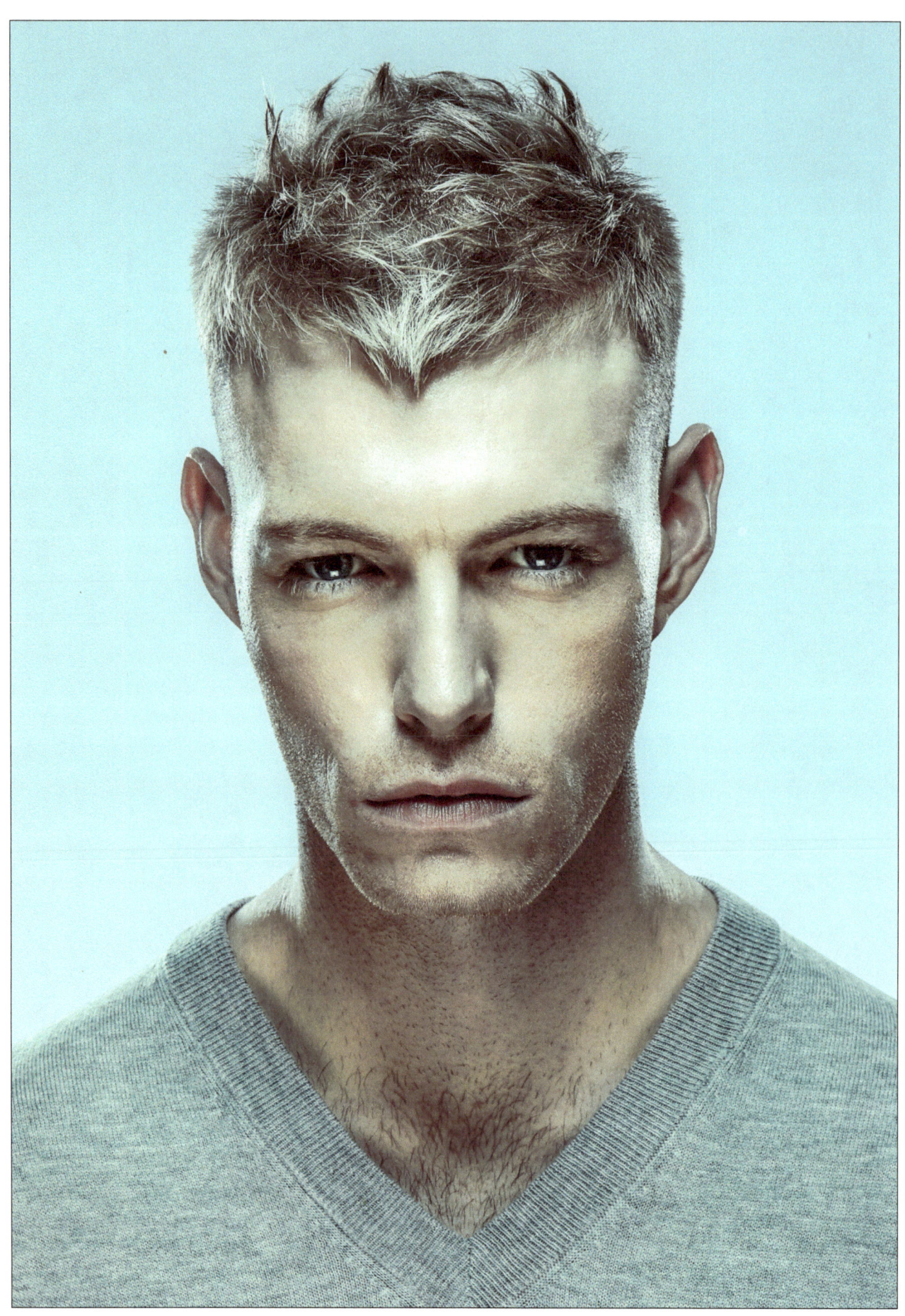

Hair: Tony Haresign - Make-up & Styling: Michelle Watson - Photography: Matt Marcus

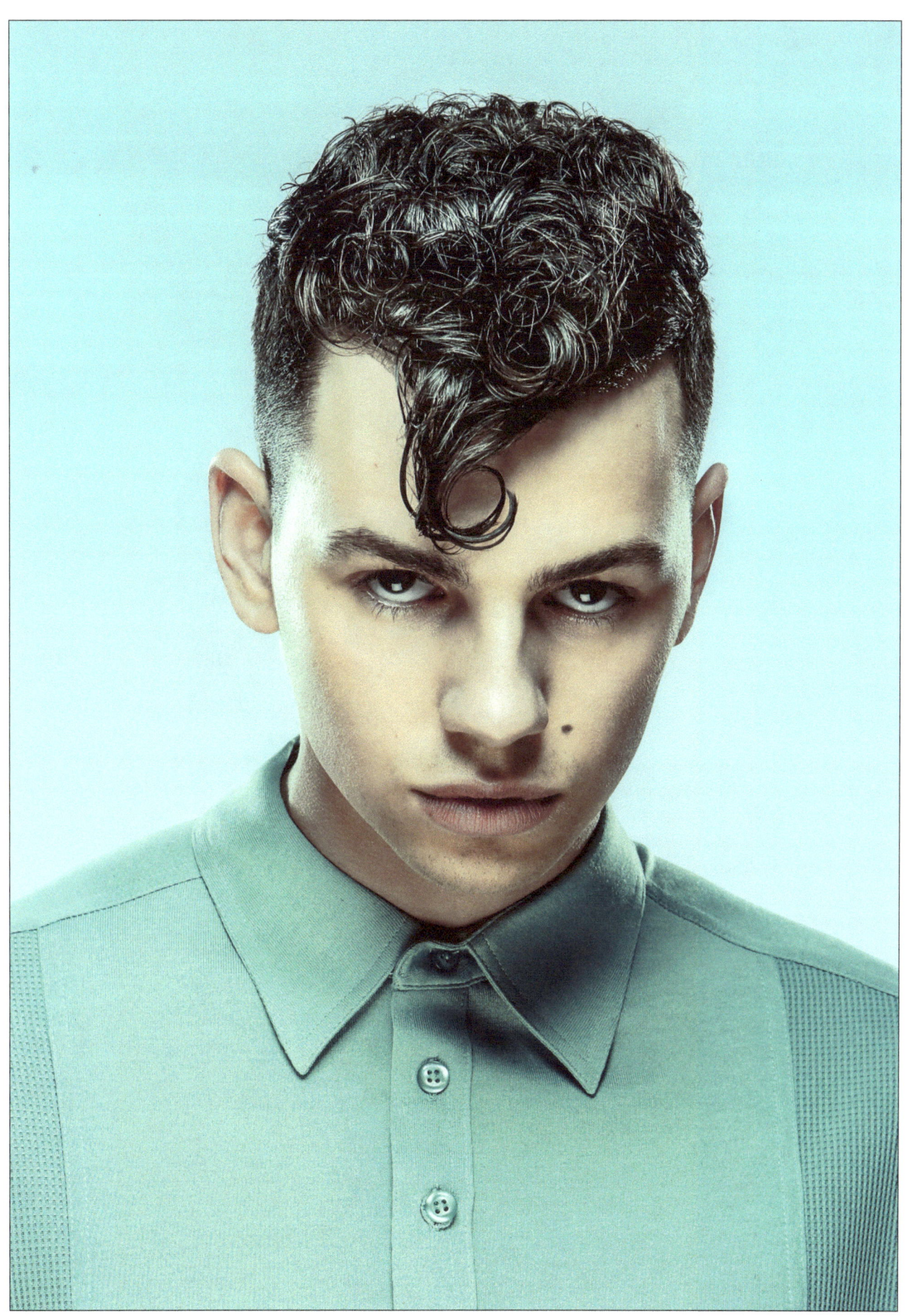

Hair: Tony Haresign - Make-up & Styling: Michelle Watson - Photography: Matt Marcus

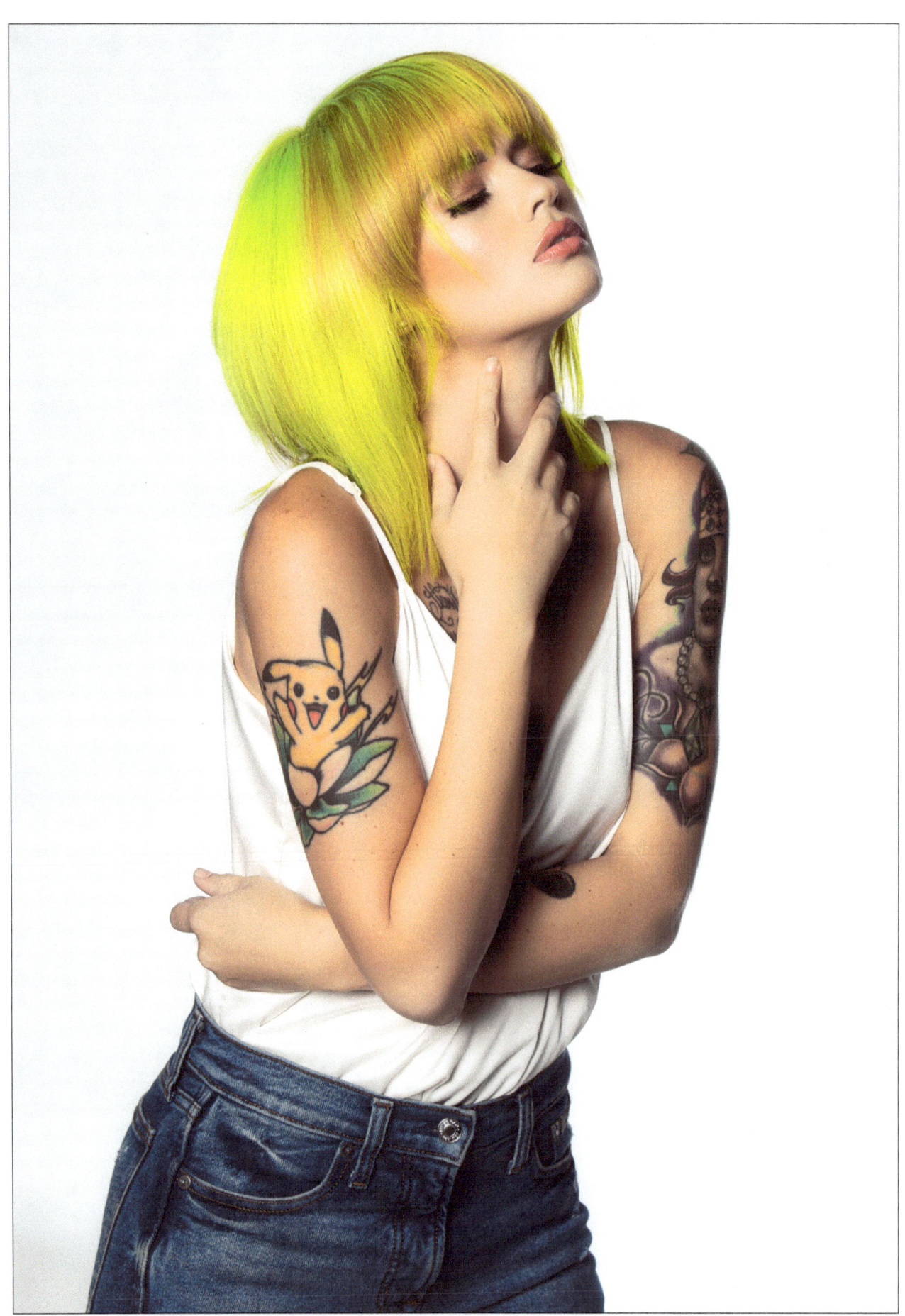

Hair: Anna Cantu & Rocky Vitelli - Make-up: Alberto Oz Caleb & Ashley Reyna - Photography: Mohammed Ghanayem

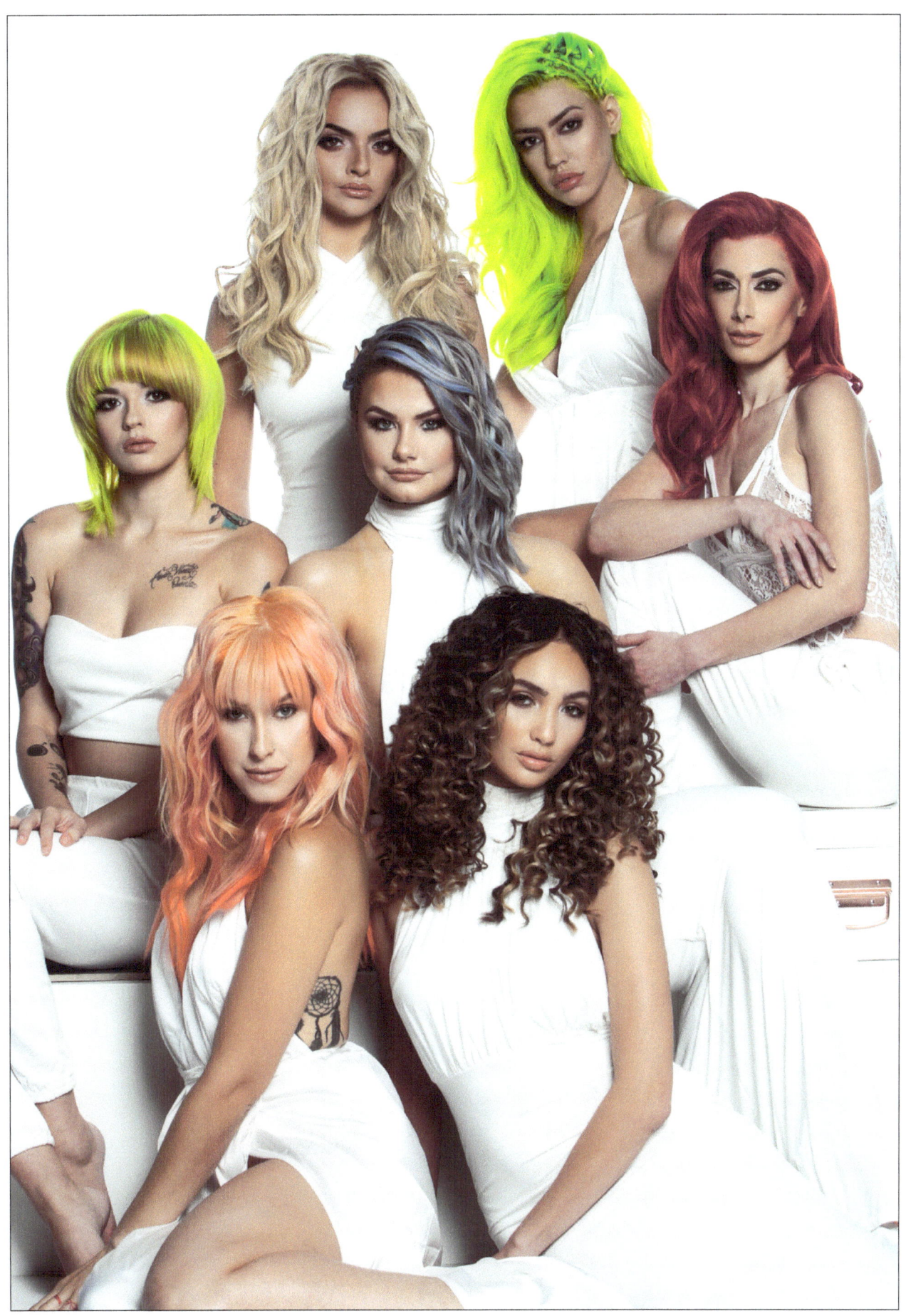

Hair: Anna Cantu & Rocky Vitelli - Make-up: Alberto Oz Caleb & Ashley Reyna - Photography: Mohammed Ghanayem

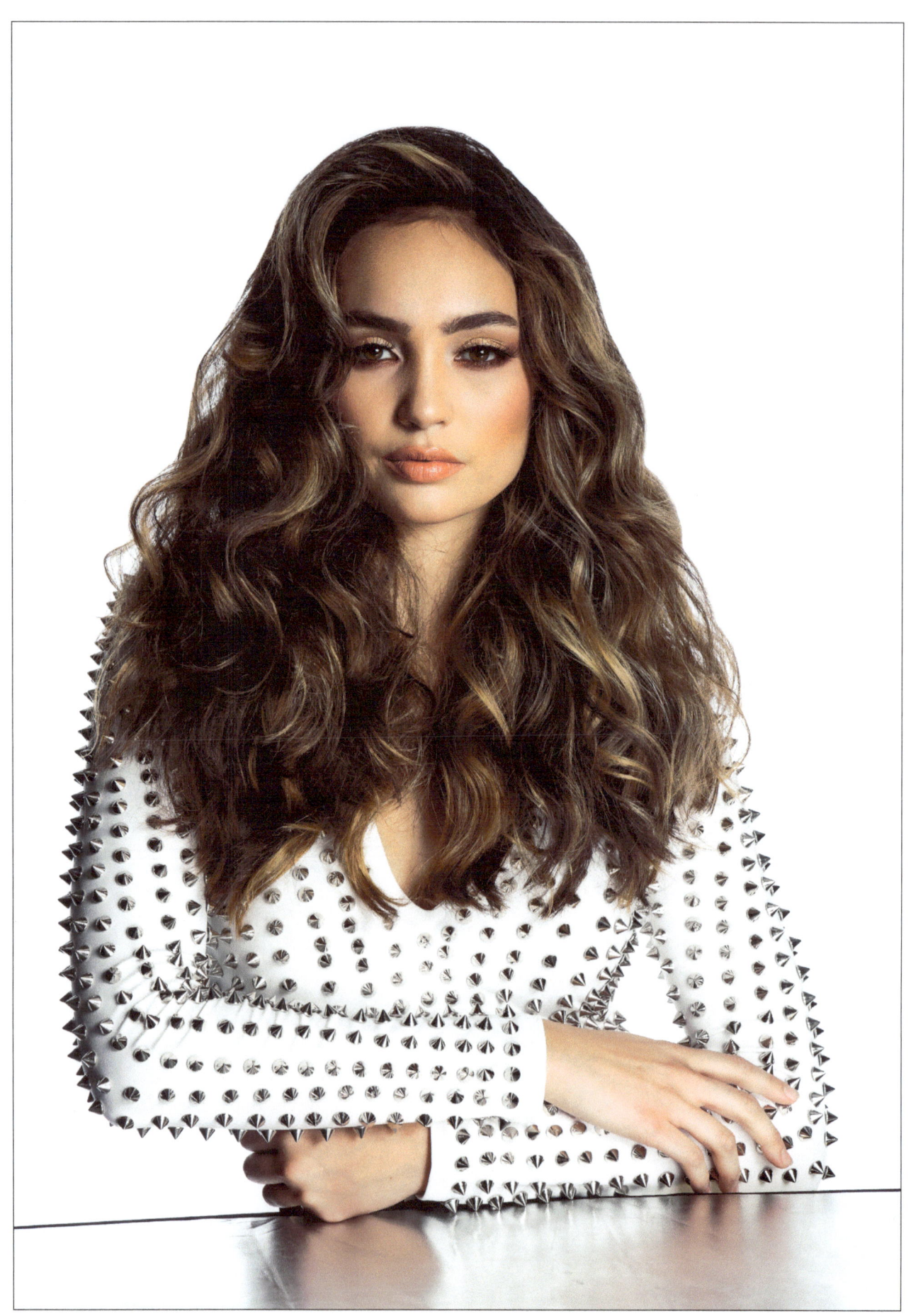

Hair: Anna Cantu & Rocky Vitelli - Make-up: Alberto Oz Caleb & Ashley Reyna - Photography: Mohammed Ghanayem

www.ingramcontent.com/pod-product-compliance
Lightning Source LLC
Chambersburg PA
CBHW051223220526
45473CB00003B/1150

9798849631370